Come Unto Me

"Drawing Near to God"

By Martha Swindle

COME UNTO ME

(Drawing Near to God)

Published by Lulu Publishers, Inc.

3131 RDU Center, Suite 210

Morrisville, NC 27560

Copyright ©2005 Martha Swindle. All rights reserved. Without prior permission of the author, no portion of this book may be reproduced.

Printed in the United States of America

ISBN 1-4116-5952-X

Scripture taken from the New King James Version®.
Copyright© 1982 by Thomas Nelson, Inc. Used by permission. All rights reserved.

I dedicate this book to my wonderful husband, Jay,
for without him this book would never have become a reality. Many
late nights I spent with the lamp on, or writing by flashlight, perched on
my pillow while he patiently slept beside me. Thank you for being so
good to me and for believing in me, but most of all for praying for me.
I love you with all my heart.

4

Table of Contents

Introduction 11
Ch. 1 - Prayer 13
Ch. 2 - My Precious Child 19
Ch. 3 - In His Gaze 23
Ch. 4 - It's Time 29
Ch. 5 - In The Valley 35
Ch. 6 - You Are Worthy, Oh Lord 39
Ch. 7 - Keep The Faith 47
Ch. 8 - Rain Down On Me 55
Ch. 9 - Greater Still 61
Ch. 10 - Fasting 67
Ch. 11 - Peace Be Still 75
Ch. 12 - Once Again 81
Ch. 13 - Praise The Lord, Amen 87
Ch. 14 - Go, Therefore 95
Ch. 15 - By His Grace I Am Free 103
Ch. 16 - His Grace 109
Ch. 17 - Come Unto Me 115
About the Author 123

6

Acknowledgements

- Momma, thank you for all the encouragement and for listening to every chapter as it was written. And for reading it over and over again when I doubted myself. I am so thankful and grateful to have a mom like you. You are the best.

- My wonderful children, Holly, Jay, and Jonathan, thank you for being so patient with me through this entire book. For helping with housework and meals, and being so flexible in when and what time we did school as a result from late nights of writing.

- My sister, Evalena, and brothers, Frank, Ronnie, and Carl, thanks for all the encouragement and for allowing me to share with others some of our special moments together.

- Zodie, Danita, Valerie, Joey, Tammy, Zoe, and Pat, my sweet sisters in Christ, thank you for all the prayers, late night calls, lunch dates, and visits that carried me through the down days of second guessing myself. Your prayers and words of encouragement carried me when I needed it most.

- Dr. Debbi Dunlap, thank you for helping me to see my potential in Christ. Thank you for all the wonderful advice that helped me get this book published. You are a precious person. Thank you for helping me to find my joy again. Blessings on your head Debbi.

- My Pastor, Eddie Pridgeon (Preacher Man). Thank you, thank you, thank you, for the sermons that I needed to hear on the days I needed to hear them most. Thank you for preaching the Truth of God's Word, all the time. I love you, Cheri, Adam, and Valerie so much.

- But most of all, I thank my Gracious Father God, Lord of my life, for loving me and for leading me throughout every page of this book. Thank You that we can go to You in prayer anytime night or day. Thank You for Jesus and for the precious gift You gave on the cross, all so that we could spend eternity in Heaven with You.

8

"With God all things are possible."

Matt. 19:26. NKJV

10

Introduction

"You need to write a book." That's what a dear friend told me years ago. I laughed at her and thought, "yeah, right" what would I possibly write about. Now look at me, here I lay in my bed 11 or 12 years later, attempting to write a book. I had always thought of being a writer when I was in high school, but I never pursued it. I didn't read lots of books and thought, "Why would I write one?" But the desire stayed tucked away in the back of my mind all this time. But even as I lay here, pen in hand, it's not me. I have been sensing the Lord telling me to write and share my heart with others, through the avenue of a book. Praise be to the Lord of Lords, and King of Kings. For only, in and through the Holy Spirit's leading could I ever pen a word. Thank you Lord Jesus.

I could never pen all the ways God has moved in my life through prayer. But in the pages ahead, I will share some testimonies and songs (or prayers to a tune) that He gave me out of my quiet time and prayer. All these songs came out of prayers. When I wrote them, it was not with the intent of writing a song. But as neat as God is, He put a tune in my heart to put with the words. The Lord knows me so well, and He knows how music moves me. So I truly believe He answers and comforts me through my prayers in song that I can remember all His promises. He speaks to my heart. Oh, how I love communing with my Father. In the pages ahead it is my desire that the Father will speak to your heart and you too will find the joy of communing with Him.

12

Chapter 1

Prayer

Prayer…I am no expert on the subject of prayer. I can only take you as far as I have been in my journey with the Lord. I don't claim to know it all, only to know the One and All. My All-Knowing, All-Powerful, Precious Lord, my Strength, and my Redeemer.

Through the simple faith of a child, I believed in Jesus Christ and started my walk with Him, it all started with a prayer. A simple, innocent, naïve prayer of a sixteen-year-old girl in her grandmother's church at a week-long revival. It went something like this…

> *Dear Father,*
> *I recognize that I am a sinner, in need of a Savior. I believe that Jesus died on the cross for my sins, was buried, and rose again on the third day, that I might have eternal life. Save me Lord today, enter my heart I pray. In Jesus' name, Amen*

A simple prayer, from a simple pray-*er*. That is all He required and let me tell you, my life has never been the same. I could tell you that life was perfect and grand and never had a bad day. But then, where would be the truth in that? Becoming a Christian was easy. Becoming Christ-like was, is, and will always be hard work.

I was not spared heartaches, disappointments, financial blunders, deaths, divorces, broken friendships, and all the other woes of life, just because I gave my heart to Christ. But through simple prayers He gave me and continues to give me unspeakable hope, grace, love, mercy, kindness, encouragement, joy, peace, and so much more.

On the days that seemed the most difficult to go through, He was there. He met me where I was and walked me throughout the entire second, minute, hour, day, week, month, and year until I was bathed in His peace. He has never sent me down a path that He has not gone ahead of me.

There are many ideas and opinions on prayer, as well as, many questions. How do I pray? What do I pray for? When do I pray? Why do I pray? There would probably be ten different answers if you were to ask ten different people. But the Father shows us in Matthew 6:1-15, how to pray. The Lord's Prayer is a model prayer for us to follow.

Our Father
(Gracious Loving Dad,
Wonderful Counselor, Meeter of our needs)

in Heaven,
(One true home.)

Hallowed be your name.
(Name above all other names)

Your kingdom come, your will be done
(Whatever you want that brings you glory Father)

On earth as it is in Heaven
(Make things here on earth the way you'd have them be)

Give us this day our daily bread
(We won't worry about tomorrow or next week,
today is sufficient for itself,
just give us what we need today…Prov. 30:8)

Forgive us our debts as we also have forgiven our debtors,
(May we be abundantly gracious to extend forgiveness to
others as we would have them to forgive us.)

And lead us not into temptation,
(Help us keep our focus on you)

but deliver us from the evil one,
(From satan and his evil schemes to destroy our witness)

***For yours is the kingdom,
and the power, and the glory forever.
Amen***
(So be it!)

There could not be a more perfect way to pray. I believe we all are intimidated at times and feel as though we do not deserve to go to God in prayer. If you believe that…Stop right now! God wants you to come to Him for everything, anytime, anywhere. He is on call 24/7. It is satan who would have you believe that your requests are unimportant to Christ. Get into the word and read all the precious promises that apply to God's children. He is so precious and worthy to be praised.

A prayer is not a routine of fancy sounding words for all to hear and say… "Oh, doesn't he or she pray beautifully?" No, prayer is just a conversation between the one praying and God Most High. Just like you would talk to a family member, friend, or spouse, is the same way you communicate with the Father. One on one. You speak, God listens. God speaks, you listen. Communion with the Father is a beautiful thing.

God so loves for us to talk to Him, with no interruptions, no being preoccupied with other things, just talk. That is why He created us, to fellowship with Him. And if we will be quiet, He loves to speak to us through His Word, communicating with our hearts. Oh, what sweet, sweet fellowship. I love it, and I love Him.

I do not always take the time to devote to prayer and unhindered communion with Him, but when I do, it is beyond comparison. When we have a conversation with others, we like to have their undivided attention. No phone ringing, no distractions, especially if we are discussing matters of importance. God wants the same thing from us…undivided attention. Ephesians 3:20 reads,

"Now to Him who is able to do exceedingly abundantly above all that we ask or think, according to the power that works in us." NKJV

According to Webster's dictionary, abundantly means - marked by great plenty; a great or rich supply. Exceedingly means - to an extreme degree. So knowing this, Eph. 3:20 reads, "Now to Him who is able with extreme degree, will richly supply above all that we ask or think according to the power that works in us." God is so awesome and able to do anything, if we would just ask according to His will.

The Lord has worked in my life so much through prayer. Sometimes I recognize the working of the Lord as it happens, sometimes after the fact. Praise the Lord that He keeps working even when I get preoccupied and forget what I prayed for. God is good and faithful and will always do what He says He will do.

In 1995, I had attended a National Women's Conference in Memphis, Tennessee. I came away from that meeting with a new vision and a desire to pray. One of the speakers encouraged us to keep a prayer journal and to look over it from time to time and see for ourselves how God answers. When I returned home I started a journal. Wow! God is awesome! He is a busy God, but He has time to listen and answer our prayers, both the complex and the simple. Even the selfish ones, you know the ones I mean. The ones that always seem to pop up before you can pray for anyone else. He is so faithful. I encourage you to keep a journal, whether you write in it daily, weekly, or hourly. Some weeks I may write in it daily, other weeks I may not touch it.

18

    I love to pray, but at times I struggle with distractions. I find that writing out my prayer keeps me focused and I am more thorough with my requests. It also keeps me grounded and from repeating the same uniform prayer over and over. It keeps me from getting in a rut. I started keeping a journal 9 years ago, and I am so glad I did. It gave me a big window to see God a little clearer. I was able to see how He works things out in His own time. Oh, dear one, what a blessing. Please try it, He desires for you to draw closer to Him.

Chapter 2

My Precious Child

Have you ever just had one of those days that everything seemed to get on your nerves? Or maybe you had a terrible outlook on life in general? I believe we all at one time or another have had one of those days. Before I ever learned to apply my spiritual armor daily, I had many days like that. One day in particular, I woke up with a chip on my shoulder. I did not open the Word or pray until bedtime that night.

All day long I seemed to run in circles. My truck was broken down and I needed to drive an hour away to get a part for it. I arrived at the dealership, received my part, went to the checkout window to pay and was ready to leave. However, when I went to pay for it, the lady behind the counter was having *one of those days.* She was hateful and rude and talked to me as if I hadn't been issued a brain at birth. So needlessly to say she *was* my topic of conversation all the way home. And the icing on the cake was when I got home, it was the wrong part. But I *"overed"* it and went on about my business, tended to my kids, talked with a friend who herself was having a trying day. I tried to encourage her to seek the Lord through her circumstances, all the while in my own mind, trying to take my own advice. All was well, I thought. That was until I crawled into bed that night and turned out the lamp and silence came.

I started to say my usual half-asleep prayer and such strong conviction came over me about my attitude that day. I could not think, nor speak my prayer without losing my train of thought. So on went the lamp, and out came the journal. I started asking God's forgiveness for my behavior and asking Him how I could have done things better. He spoke such sweet and forgiving words to my heart and told me how I could have spoken a word of encouragement to the dear lady who was obviously having a horrid day. Then satan put his two cents in about how no good I am for the Lord. That nothing I do is good enough. It was then that the Lord had me turn the page in my journal and just write what He told me to. I was not sure what He wanted, but I did as He told me. I turned the page and these are the words He had me pen.

My Precious Child

As I lay here tonight, thinking about this day,
What could I have done better? Did I turn anyone away?
From seeing the love of Christ, or feeling His precious touch,
Maybe helping them with a burden,
that seemed a little too much.

Then I heard Him say…
My child, you pleased Me, more than you'll ever know.
You kissed your child's hurt away, you hugged a wounded soul.
You lifted up your burdens, then you gently let them go,
You came to Me, I filled you up,
Well Done, My precious child.

I couldn't believe what I heard, was this me He was speaking of?
With all the thoughts and feelings I had,
that didn't reflect His love.
Though all the ways I fail Him, He still loves me so,
He takes what little I can do, and blesses my heart and soul.

My child, you pleased Me, more than you'll ever know.
I'll kiss your every hurt away; I'll hug your wounded soul.
Come to Me, I'll fill you up, and every burden I'll take away,
As you run the race before you, until you hear Me say,
Well Done, My precious child.

The kindness He has shown me, His love so pure and true,
What else could I offer? What else could I do?
I could ask you if you know Him,
have you called upon His name?
If so, then my beloved, you will hear Him say…

My child, you pleased Me, more than you'll ever know,
I'll kiss your every hurt away; I'll hug your wounded soul.
Come to Me, I'll fill you up, and every burden I'll take away.
And when your final days are through, you will hear me say…
Well Done, Welcome home, My precious child.

Several weeks prior to writing these words, I caught myself humming an unfamiliar tune. I kept trying to figure where I had heard the song before. On more than one occasion I would find myself humming it over and over. It would mainly be while I washed dishes, folded clothes; household chores that took time to do. Never did I realize what was taking place.

When I started writing the words in my journal, that unfamiliar tune came to me and I wrote the words out in rhythm to the tune. I remembered thinking, "Where is this coming from?" I knew what was happening, but I was awestruck. It challenged me to finish. I had two verses and a chorus within five minutes; I spent about fifteen more minutes on the last verse. It was so amazing, I talked to the Lord and He spoke to me in song. I truly was in worship as I had never experienced before.

By the time I was to write the third verse, I started telling the Father – "Your kindness You have shown, Your love so pure and true. What could I ever offer? What more could I do?" And He just spoke to my heart, "Ask others if they know me, ask them if they will call upon my name." I truly did not write this song. It was a very precious intimate moment with my Savior, one on one. I spoke, He listened; He spoke, I listened.

Washing the dishes took on a new meaning from that day forward. At the end of not-so-great days, the Lord has given me a song; a wonderful reminder…of His unconditional love. If I had the means and was in your neighborhood, I would sing you a tune. These promises were not given just for me. You too are His precious child. We are God's pleasures, God's treasures; rest in Him today.

Chapter 3

In His Gaze

How many times have you tried to do things in your own strength and not relied on God? Mine are more than I can count. I always seem to go and go until the brick wall hits me right between the eyes. It is then that reality sets in and I have my little mini-revelation of, "I just can't do this anymore." Hello! Been there?

I have had many a day just like that. But I have become more and more dependent on the Lord for His strength and endurance in raising my family, managing my finances, my marriage, and more. In prayer He has shown me my need for Him. If we never take the time to pray, then we will never grow any closer to Him, nor will we become more Christ-like. Through reading scripture and talking to Him on a daily basis, we start walking in His strength and in less of our own strength.

I encourage you to read Ephesians 6:10-19, every morning when you wake and every evening before you go to bed, putting on the full armor of God, night and day. For when things seem difficult and hard to bear and we are not grounded in His word, and protected by His promises, then satan gets a foothold. Ephesians 6:12 reads,

> *"For we do not wrestle against flesh and blood, but against principalities, against powers, against the rulers of the darkness of this age, against spiritual hosts of wickedness in the heavenly places." NKJV*

Satan is up 24/7, thinking up ways to trip us up in our walk with the Lord. He knows our weaknesses and he uses those areas to get to us. That is why we can do nothing in our own strength, for we are weak sinful people. But through God's grace and mercy we have strength to face life's most difficult blows, whether it is broken relationships, finances, physical, mental, or verbal abuse. God's strength is made perfect in our weakness. Scripture reads in 2 Corinthians 2:9,

> *"My grace is sufficient for you, for My strength is made perfect in weakness." NKJV*

I have been to the altar at church many times over broken dreams, broken promises, and broken hearts. I have hurt and grieved over the death of dear loved ones. I have wept many a day over my children and my marriage. When I feel at my lowest, I go to the church when no one is around and cry out for Jesus' intercessory prayer.

> *"Likewise the Spirit also helps in our weaknesses. For we do not know what we should pray for as we ought, but the Spirit Himself makes intercession for us with groanings which cannot be uttered. Now He who searches the hearts knows what the mind of the Spirit is, because He makes intercession for the saints according to the will of God."*   *Romans 8:26-27, NKJV*

We can pray anywhere, anytime, but sometimes I just feel compelled to lie at the altar at His feet and weep and beg for mercy and peace. That is when those mountains start to crumble and the dark clouds fade away. One on one, I cry out, and God listens. He hears our every cry and He knows every tear that falls from our eyes. He loves us with such abundant love. He is there always, waiting for our call. So, if you are burdened, get alone with God, seek forgiveness for any known or unknown sin, and then just start talking. He will meet you where you are, you can see your reflection in His gaze.

In His Gaze

*As I knelt at the altar for prayer,
I was burdened with a load of care.
I came seeking refuge, from the world and its ways,
And what I found there was my reflection in His gaze.*

*He told me child, I've been waiting for your call,
I've been praying to My Father, make you strong,
I heard your cries; I felt your pain,
But most of all, I bore your shame.
Come to me, here I am, find rest.*

*My tears could not I contain,
my brokenness was all I could claim,
He knew me better than I ever knew myself,
I claimed victory over satan,
fought my battle, kept the faith,
I met my Savior in the reflection of His gaze.*

*He told me child, I've been waiting for your call,
I've been praying to My Father, make you strong,
I heard your cries; I felt your pain,
But most of all, I bore your shame,
Come to me, here I am, find rest.*

*So dear friend, let me say, it can be yours too this day.
Take your stand, call on Jesus, and be saved.
He bore your cross, He paid the price,
He was the Perfect Sacrifice.
Come and see your reflection in His gaze.*

*He tells us child, I've been waiting for your call.
I've been praying to My Father, make them strong.
I heard your cries, I felt your pain,
But most of all, I bore your shame,
Come to Me, here I am, find rest.*

The night this prayer came to life in a song, was after a wonderful gospel sing. I was a member of a gospel group and we were opening for another group at a local church. Weeks prior to the sing our group had been experiencing growing pains. We loved one another dearly, but we had been having some differences that at the time were taking a toll on me. Minor differences as they were, my life in general seemed to be spiraling out of control. Our finances were not in the best of shape, the tremendous responsibility of raising three kids, not to mention homeschooling, my marriage, I was struggling. To look at me on the outside, I had it all together. But on the inside I was buckling under pressure.

The night of singing was a wonderful dose of therapy. Singing His praises lifted my spirit and the other group was a blessing to me as well. I worshipped in my heart and with hands raised. It was a beautiful time. After all the singing was over, the preacher gave an altar call and had taken several prayer requests. As people made their way to the altar to pray, I suddenly found myself kneeling on the padded altar. I went to pray for a certain request I had heard, the next thing I knew I was unloading my woes to the Lord, right then and there. Not even minding that this was not my home church, definitely out of my comfort zone.

I started crying almost heaving, when all at once I felt someone's hand rest on my shoulder, then several. And a lady's voice I started to hear. She started praying over me and I am here to tell you, she laid it on the altar for me. We knew each other, but not personally. She prayed specifically about our group, praying satan would not hinder us, then she pinpointed and prayed about things that only God and I knew about. I do not mean exact details, but I mean she touched on every aspect I was dealing with.

Chills went up and down my spine – she was as fervent in prayer for me as if it was all happening to her personally. Healing started taking place in my heart at that very moment. It was as if someone gave me oxygen and removed shackles from my body.

When we were through and I raised my head, I was surrounded by others in my group; they had gone to the altar on their own as well. Several members of the church had surrounded us and laid hands on one another as we all prayed. I looked like a big, slobbery baby. Boohooing all over the place, but I had been set free.

With amazement I looked up at the dear lady who had prayed, and asked her, "How did you know what I needed?" She just smiled and said, "He told me." I came home on such a spiritual high. My soul had been fed. As I lay in bed and pondered what all took place that night, I began humming and writing…as I knelt at the altar for prayer. Within fifteen to thirty minutes, God had spoke to me once again through a tune, words that I desperately needed to hear. "Come to Me, here I AM, find rest."

Chapter 4

It's Time

Today's world is moving at such a loud, busy pace. Each day runs into the next, like a roller coaster that never stops. It is so easy to get caught up in the worldly ways. From cars, houses, vacations, recreation, to so much more, it is easy to lose our focus and leave God out of the picture.

Life is all about choices. We either serve Him or serve the world. I have been caught doing both. Guess what…it does not work. God's Word says:

> *"No servant can serve two masters; for either he will hate the one and love the other, or else he will be loyal to the one and despise the other. You cannot serve God and mammon."*
> *Luke 16:13, NKJV*

There is no possible way to do both. I took a gut check and realized that I had to start making better choices. I need not compare myself to others, I do not need everything, be it job, money, or whatever.

We were created for two things, to fellowship with God and to tell others about Jesus who lives in the hearts of those who call upon His name. Life is not about us, it is all about God. We need to take every opportunity to share the love of Christ with others. Sharing is not limited to just telling others the plan of salvation. It is showing love to that neighbor who is hard to love, teaching a Sunday School class, discipling someone whose faith in the Lord is new and mentoring them in their walk with Christ. Sharing Christ's love is dying to yourself and living for Christ.

In the early years of my marriage we struggled off and on with our finances. At the time, my husband worked for a construction company who paid well, but every September or October they would lay people off until January or February. We knew this, yet Jay continued to work for them for we live in a small town without many jobs. Being young and not knowing much about budgeting, we fell into hard times. Our parents on several occasions bought us groceries, helped pay utility bills, bought diapers, etc. We both worked, but with debt occurred and fluctuating paychecks, we struggled to make ends meet.

I can remember lying awake at nights, trying to figure in my head what all I could pay with this paycheck. What can wait until next paycheck? I started praying, pretty much pleading with the Lord, "give me, give me, please, what I need to pay our bills." All I heard was silence, not one miracle could I see, or so I thought.

My girlfriend, on day a couple of years before this night, had shared with me what tithing meant. She told me the story of God and ten apples. She said, "Martha, God gives you ten beautiful, sweet, red, delicious apples. He gives them all to you freely. All He asks that you give Him one apple back. All He wants is one, you keep the other nine. That is tithing a tenth of what He gives you." I was amazed. I had been going to church for three or four years and never had I heard it put in such a way. The pastor would preach on money from time to time, but it never dawned on me that I should tithe my income. Over the next year or two, I would think about tithing, but I would stop myself saying, "There is no way I could tithe. I have a hard time making ends meet now, much less tithe." I know it was the Lord prompting me off and on, but I dug my heels in the dirt, and plugged along.

One night during my pleading prayer time, the silence was broken. But not with the words I thought I would hear. Instead of the Lord saying, yes to my give me, give me, for my bills plea…He said, "No, give them to me."

"What Lord? What do You mean give them to You?"

"I want your tithe, and bills, I'll do the rest."

"Lord, I can't, how will I pay bills?"
"You won't, I will."

"Lord…"

"Martha…do you trust me?"

"Yes Lord."

I was speechless. I tried to ration in my mind, "How will this work?" Then His words would ring in my ears… *"Trust me."* I started tithing and just paid what I could, when I could. There was not instant cash flow. We still had past due bills, collection calls, kids to raise, gas and groceries to buy, light bills, phone bills, car payments, etc. Nothing had changed except my heart. I knew He would take care of me one day at a time, one second at a time on my worst days. I had peace for the first time in a long time.

I was growing closer and closer to the Lord. I would love to be able to tell you that I have tithed faithfully ever since, but that would be a lie. I have faltered many times and taken my eyes off God, even until this day. It has been a process, an area that I have been disciplined by the Master many times. When I fail to tithe, the Lord allows me to go on my own for awhile, then He always gets my attention in some way and steers me back to Him. I am at peace when I tithe. God is gracious to extend forgiveness and gives me a fresh start. In Malachi 3:10, scripture tells us to test God in our tithes and offerings, and we will see Him pour out the blessings. It is true, oh so true, but selfishness takes root at times and I try to start handling things on my own.

Through this whole process, I started learning that money is not the answer. The cares of this world pale in comparison to the glory of the Lord. He loves us, He tells us in His Word that He has gone to prepare a place for His children who have called upon His name. And one day when our place, our mansion is ready, He will call us home to Him.

I started making decisions based on what God wanted, not me. With questions and eyebrows raised from some friends and family, I had a third child when my kids were ten and seven. I became a stay-at-home mom, even homeschooling, for as long as God wants me too. Never in my realm of thinking did I believe I would be able to stay at home, we always needed two incomes. But God blessed as He promised, maybe not always in monetary ways, but blessings and provisions all the same. Jay and I started living for Christ and trusted Him in the big and small things. I quit worrying about what people thought of me and started trusting God more. At times, I struggle with other peoples opinions of me, but I have to remind myself, trust, trust, trust, in the One who knows best.

Whether you stay-at-home, work, married or single, the only one we need to measure ourselves by is Christ. He will make a way, when there doesn't seem to be a way. We just need to be willing vessels, sharing His love with others and encouraging them through debilitating circumstances.

There have been many times that I have stumbled and fell and started looking to the world for peace. But God is faithful to forgive and give do-*overs* daily. Only Christ can give the peace that passes all understanding. It's time we take a stand as believers in Christ and allow Him to work His perfect work in and through us until He comes back to take us home. Praise the Lord.

It's Time

I may not have the mansion most men dream of,
I may not drive the car of the day,
But I hold to the promise, that He is always there,
To lead and to guide me, every step of the way.

He's gone to prepare, me a place,
And to call me home on high,
So I'll stand firm, and His praises daily sing,
Until He says it's time.

Sometimes I compare myself to others,
I ask what use could I be.
Then he gently reminds me,
Just follow, repent, and believe.

He's gone to prepare, me a place,
And to call me home on high,
So I'll stand firm, and His praises daily sing,
Until He says it's time.

We are only willing vessels,
To be used according to His will,
To share His saving power with others,
And to tell them with His spirit be filled.

He's gone to prepare, You a place,
And to call You home on high,
So just stand firm, and His praises daily sing,
Until He says it's time.

He's gone to prepare, me a place,
And to call me home on high,
So I'll stand firm, and His praises daily sing,
Until He says it's time

Chapter 5

In The Valley

Valleys, at the time, can be the most difficult thing we ever had to endure and be a time we just as soon forget. However, in the long run, I often realize it was the most beautiful time in my life. I have had my share of low times and I am certain there are many more to come. But I have come to learn that it is in those lowest points in life that God is teaching me more about His character.

His love is so amazing. He loves us with such a deep, sincere, unhindered, unconditional love. And He is fully aware of everything we go through. He wants us to grow in our faith and become more and more like Him, and one of the ways we can do that is to show our complete dependence on Him. When things are going great and smooth and there are no kinks in the road, I tend to lose sight of what God has called me to do. But in those valley's, yea, that is where the rubber meets the road. That is where I have the opportunity to put my so called "faith" into action. When things are difficult and unclear is when I have to trust God in blind faith. That is when He will provide money for bills, healing for the hurt, peace for the harried, wisdom for the clueless, sanctuary in the storm. God is so powerful and so awesome and could make life perfect so we would never have problems. But then, we would never have to trust Him. Every trial, every burden, every heartache, is a part of God's plan to grow us closer to Him. In James 1:2-4 the Bible reads,

> *"Count it all joy when you fall into various trials, knowing that the testing of your faith produces patience. But let patience have its perfect work, that you may be complete, lacking nothing."*

Do you see the beauty there? He wants us to be complete and lacking nothing. He only wants the best for us. Yes, valleys hurt, but oh, the beauty that comes from the ashes. We serve a compassionate and merciful God and He will never put more on us than we can bear. The deepest valleys make the greatest mountain tops even more beautiful than we could ever imagine.

I have struggled off and on in my own life, be it my marriage, my children, my finances and more. But I am learning that when I find myself in a valley, to start looking around and ask the Lord…what do you want me to learn from this situation? The Bible says:

> *"No temptation has overtaken you except such that is common to man; but God is faithful, who will not allow you to be tempted beyond what you are able, but with temptation will also make the way of escape, that you may be able to bear it."*
> *1 Corinthians 10:13, NKJV*

The Father is faithful and will always have a window open where a door is closed. He knows what is best for us.

When my dad died, I was devastated. I hurt a hurt that I never knew I could hurt. It was hard to see the lesson God wanted me to learn. But even though my dad's life ended here on earth, eternity in Heaven was His great reward, for He knew the Lord. At that time, all my family but one brother had accepted the Lord and was saved. But something beautiful took place the weekend daddy passed away. Through my dad's death, my brother's heart was softened and he gave his heart to Christ that weekend. To this day his life was forever changed and he has a deep love for the Lord. The even neater part of it is that my other brother led him to the Lord. Awesome! Priceless. All that beauty came from one of the darkest times of my life. I now have the peace and security knowing that my entire family will be reunited in Heaven.

Dear Gracious Father,

Thank you for reminding me of the beauty that takes place in the valleys I go through. You are my Rock and my Fortress and my Ever-Present Help in times of trouble. I love you Lord. In Jesus' name,

Amen

In The Valley

Oh the valley is a road often traveled,
Where our fears and our weaknesses lie,
It's there He meets us on our journey,
And it's there; He's right by our side

It's in the valley I learn more about Him,
It's in the valley I long to see His face,
It's in the valley I gain more understanding,
It's in the valley I learn how to lean.

At times I am discouraged and downhearted,
And I question, "Oh, Lord, why must this be?"
Then He gently whispers to me,
It's in the valleys you draw close to me.

It's in the valley I learn more about Him,
It's in the valley I long to see His face,
It's in the valley I gain more understanding,
It's in the valley I learn how to lean.

So don't look at the valley as a burden,
But see it for what it's meant to be,
A place of worship for His children,
To get a glimpse of our Savior and King.

It's in the valley I learn more about Him,
It's in the valley I long to see His face,
It's in the valley I gain more understanding,
It's in the valley I learn how to lean.

Chapter 6

You Are Worthy, Oh Lord

As you probably can tell by now, I have been through some valleys. I have had a good dose of knowing the feeling of despair. I have had pity party after pity party over things of the simplest nature. And then I've had true valleys that I felt justified in being in. More than not, my personal valleys were a result of sin. No, I have not killed anyone, committed adultery, nor robbed a bank. Disobedience has been my valley. That is, and seems to continue at times to be my biggest obstacle.

The sin of disobedience reaps consequences that tend to last. Choosing to buy now, pay later led me into the trap of financial "yuck". Choosing to react instead of act in discussions with my kids and husband led me to say hurtful things to them, which in turn left me and them feeling horrible. Choosing to start my day without spending time with the Lord, led me to walk in my own strength and fall into an attitude of burn-out and pure exhaustion. But the biggest and foremost important one is that I choose to allow sin to put up a wall between the Lord and me, shielding His face and blessings from me. Disobedience can result from many things; not tithing on the money He has entrusted us, poor management of money, or not doing those things which He may have called us to do. Such as, teaching, singing, witnessing, or serving Him in some capacity. These are all forms of disobedience.

When we neglect to make time for God, we are failing to serve Him and we are hindering our walk with Him. He is worthy to be praised and we should be about His business, and offering up our praises daily. When we do not make time to get directions from the Lord, we give satan that foothold once again. We allow satan the opportunity to sap our time and energy. So when I stumble and fall; it gives me a chance to look up and see my need for God, my need to repent and seek His forgiveness, my need to praise Him and give Him the honor and glory due Him. For He alone is worthy to be praised.

Several years ago I found myself severely discontented in my marriage. I was tired of feeling like I was the only one that did anything around the house. Jay and I seemed to be on opposite sides of the page, bickering and fussing more often than not. I was lonely and longed for Jay's undivided attention. I knew he loved me, but I wanted more. I wanted to be told more often how much he loved me. At least more than what he was doing at the time, or so I thought. I wanted to be the center of all his affection and attention. It may sound selfish and it was, but at the same time, I needed reassurance of his love and commitment to me. I truly felt like a doormat, just to be used as needed.

I went to work on a Wednesday morning after a really long, long night of no sleep and wishing things were better. I was confused and torn, absolutely miserable. Jay must have thought I was losing my mind and it felt like I was doing just that. My employer at the time, a very godly man, came through my office and noticed my downcast spirit. He offered words of encouragement and reminded me of all Jay's good points that he knew to be true. I thanked him for his words of advice but told him that I needed some time think about everything. I was in no shape to work, I asked him if I could leave for the day, and to have Thursday and Friday off as well. (Surely, not asking too much on the spur of the moment, haha.) He allowed me to leave.

      I spent the afternoon planning and mulling over in my mind what I was doing. I did not want to leave my husband, but yet, I could not stay like things were. I called my girlfriend and asked if I could use her beach house for a couple of days that I needed some time alone to think. She said yes, and encouraged me to seek the Lord with all my heart. She lent me some tapes with a message about "Hearing God", and I started collecting my thoughts. My kids were still in public school at that time.

      Thursday morning, I talked with the kids before school and told them that daddy would be picking them up from school and that I would be gone for a couple of days. I told them that I loved them very much and that I loved their daddy, but that I needed to be alone with God. I prayed with them and took them on to school. I came back home and packed my truck: sleeping bag, pillow, blanket, flash light, clothes, bible, journal, tape player, Christian music, and a few groceries. I then went to where Jay was working in town and told him that he would need to get the kids home from school and see about them. I told him that I was going to stay at the beach for a couple of days to decide if I still wanted to be married, and suggested that he think about it too. And I left.

I arrived at the beach house, and settled in. It was so quiet. I remember sitting thinking to myself, "What in the world are you doing here? How did you get to this point?" I had my pity party going full force. Me, myself, and I…what a group we were. We were all in agreement that I needed to leave, that it was over. I would walk down to the water and sit and look out over the ocean, wondering what to do. My heart felt as though it were being ripped from my chest.

Back at the house, I listened to music and then I would sit in absolute silence. "Lord, why can't I hear You?" I would say. I opened my Bible expecting some great revelation. Nothing was revealed to me. Then I wandered back down to the shore line and sat there for what seemed like forever. I must have looked pitiful. The beautiful scene of the ocean faded into the night, and I retreated back to the house and readied myself for bed. I sprawled out on the bed with my Bible, journal, music, radio, all the things I thought I would need to find my answer. About 2:00 a.m., after spending hours listening to tapes, reading, praying, pitying myself, I broke. Tears rushed down my face, I cried out…

> *"Lord, what is going on? I am hurting so. I am nothing without You. I so desperately want to be the wife You want me to be, but I don't know if I have what it takes to try anymore. What is wrong with me? Why aren't You hearing me? What am I to do? How will I raise my kids alone? What? I hurt so badly. I want Jay to love me. I want him to spend quality time with me. I am tired of begging him for his attention."*

I was sobbing for what seemed forever, and then I just hushed and laid there in a trance. I was so sleepy, yet I could not sleep. I was out of words, completely spent. Then it came. Those sweet, still gentle words of my Loving Savior.

> *"Martha, I hear your cries. I know what you are saying, but do not act in haste. All these things you tell Me you want from Jay…I want from you. Undivided attention, quality time, one on one, I long for that relationship with you. Do you see what I am saying My child? The difference is, not once did I want to leave you. I am patient, I will wait on you to come to me, I will love you until you love me that way."*

I just sat there in complete shock. I was so convinced that is was all about Jay and I, not once did I think it was about the Lord and I.

> *"I long to spend time with You Lord, but I get so busy. You know I love You."*
>
> *"Jay longs to spend more time with you, but he too is busy, and you know he loves you."*
>
> *"I want you to change him Lord. Make him the husband I need him to be."*
>
> *"I want to change you Martha, love him unconditionally. Dote over him and make him feel as special as you can."*

"What? Lord, this isn't fair. It isn't all my fault that our marriage is struggling right now."

"This may be true, but you are the one here seeking Me, are you willing to be the one to change?"

I awoke in the morning right where I was amidst my pile of treasures in the middle of the bed. Thinking about the events that took place in the wee hours, I made some breakfast and ate in complete silence. Again, making my trek down to the water line, I peered out across the vast ocean thinking once again, "What am I doing here? How did I get to this point?" I felt God's leading but at the same time, I started resenting what He had told me. I spent the next couple of hours sitting there, almost arguing with God. It was about Jay, not me. It was about our marriage, not my relationship to the Lord. This weekend is about God restoring my marriage, not restoring me. What was happening here?

Back at the house, I continued to jump back and forth between my head and my heart. Satan was glorifying in the moment. He had me right where he wanted me, on the verge of a divorce. Disillusioned, almost fooled into thinking that a divorce was needed, and that reconciliation was impossible. I dug my heels in deep trying to plead my case, but to no avail.

It was dark once again, and I perched up in the bed, determined to make God see my side once again. My stubbornness was waning. Every thought that I could muster, the Lord had an answer to. Finally, I said, "Yes, Lord. Not my will but thine." I cried and asked His forgiveness; true repentance took place in my heart. Sudden relief and peace came upon my heart. I was free, no longer a prisoner of my mind. What started as a weekend all about Jay, ended in a weekend all about me. I committed to put God first above all things, and that I would be the wife to Jay that God wanted me to be. I thanked Him for growing me through the whole ordeal.

    I started packing up my things and at 11:30 p.m. I was walking in my front door. I was happy, giddy, revived. Jay's face was priceless. He could not figure me out I know. I loved on my kids and put them in bed. Then I told Jay how sorry I was and that I would never ever leave again. I told him that the Lord done business with me over the past two days and that I knew without a doubt that I wanted to be married for a long, long time. He and I both talked for the longest time and asked each other for forgiveness. Painful, yet one of the most beautiful times, a new beginning was started.

    God is so wonderful, so gracious, so loving. He is worthy of all honor and praise. I learned that in a most humbling way. I thank Him all the time for Jay. I have been blessed with a truly wonderful husband. To think back today, I think how silly it must have looked. But I know that God had greater plans for our marriage. He knew the opposition we would face in the years ahead and He has and will continue to equip us.

    All this said for a lesson well learned. God longs for our praises, on our own. He never gives up on us, and He always loves us unconditionally. When we praise Him daily He loves us, when we forget Him for days, He still loves us.

You Are Worthy, Oh Lord

You are worthy Oh Lord, of honor and praise.
You order my life, my night and my day.

No problem too big, no request too small,
You stand ready and waiting, to move in them all.

You are worthy Oh Lord, of honor and praise.
You order my life, my night and my day.

Fully aware, of each step I will take.
Always protecting, for my sake.

You are worthy Oh Lord, of honor and praise.
You order my life, my night and my day.

Thank you dear God, for creation so grand.
Help me draw close to You, give me courage to stand.

You are worthy Oh Lord, of honor and praise.
You order my life, my night and my day.

You order my life…My night and my day.

Chapter 7

Keep the Faith

Keeping the faith? What does that mean? That means that when all is chaos, all is uncertain, all seems too stressful, all seems impossible, and all is just…too much - we totally and completely give it all to the Lord, knowing that He knows best. There are times when it seems as though things will never get better. There are times when life just seems too impossible to survive with any sanity. And there are times when we feel so totally alone. You would think that as big as the world is and with as many inhabitants that we would not feel alone. But it happens. You can have the most friends, the closest family, the best church family, the greatest so called "have it all" life, and be the loneliest person you know.

I am a living testimony to that fact. I would say for the past two years, I have been lonelier than ever imaginable. I have just recently, probably within the last four to five months, climbed out of a valley that I thought would never end. I was spent, my energy was depleted. I did not want to go anywhere, nor be in public places. To get out of bed in the mornings was a challenge.

I would pray and it would seem like God was no where to be found. I could not hear Him speak, I could not feel His presence, I felt emotionally, physically, and spiritually drained.

I remember telling my husband one night as we were lying in bed talking, "Jay, I don't even want to get up in the mornings. I just want to hide from the world and stay in the bed." He then told me that he has days like that, but that he makes himself get out of bed and go to work and not give in to satan's schemes. He told me that I needed to make myself get up, for satan was working on my thoughts, and he reminded me how much the Lord loved me and that satan was not happy with my relationship and witness for the Lord. So I did...and it worked...for that day. But I soon was back in the same frame of mind.

I was going through the motions, opening my Bible, reading a verse, saying a prayer, going to church, smiling on the outside while downcast on the inside, walking along as if nothing was wrong. I prayed and asked God what was wrong with me, what was I doing wrong, was I doing anything right? Silence... that is what I heard. I could not understand why He was not telling me what I wanted to hear. I kept thinking, hmm, my direct line must have lots of static in it. Here I was...Martha, the so-called, "spiritual one", "faithful one", "always-has- an-encouraging-word-to-say-one", "always-has-it-together-one", struggling. But I dare not tell anyone how I was feeling, for then I might look weak and untrusting in God. So I just became stagnant, withdrawn to myself, and ready to give up. I kept praying faithfully to the Lord about my situation, knowing that He was still in control, and knew what was best for my life.

Then one morning, I was lying in bed, later than I should have been, flipping through the channels on the television (I had the remote to myself, haha), and I flipped to a commercial; one of those commercials for anti-depressants. They listed the symptoms of depression on the screen and I read probably 7 out of 8 that I had. MERCY!! That was it, I was suffering from depression. I diagnosed myself, whew! Glad I figured that one out, didn't even need the doctor to tell me that one. I jumped up out of bed, got dressed, and went walking. I thought to myself, I do not want to take medication for depression, I'll walk this off. You should have seen me, strutting down the street looking half-crazed, walking, praying and praising the Lord that I was cured of this here depression business. It was a hoot!

It worked for a couple of weeks, but then I was right back into the same blah, blah, mood. Over this same time period of the blahs, I had been suffering from nightmares. They were nightmares of spiritual warfare, with my rebuking satan in my dreams, and I would wake up scared to death. My dreams were so real, so vivid. Several weeks later, the depression seemed to be back on me full force. Sleepless nights were once again wearing me down.

I remember one night feeling completely spent, or at "rock bottom" as the saying goes. I lay there thinking all kinds of stupid thoughts, and I could not get to sleep. I was miserable. I kept thinking about my family (was I a good enough mom, wife, teacher), my friends (do they still like me, have I done anything to offend them), my church (I had stop teaching, singing, basically quit participating in any activity, worried about what everyone thought of me). Finally, I just got up, went to my closet, shut the door, knelt down at my rocker, and began to cry, uncontrollable blubbering crying.

I started telling the Father, how my heart was broken, how I was nothing without Him, and that I could no longer keep up this image that I had made for myself. That I needed Him more than I ever had before, and told Him that I was tired of going through the motions. I just cried and cried.

After a while the crying ceased and everything was quiet. I began to moan. But it was kind of weird, hard to explain. I was on the floor, feet folded under me, with my hands in the rocker seat. My whole body was rocking back and forth, as I moaned. A low, peaceful moan…I could not speak, nor cry. It seemed to last forever, but in reality probably 30 minutes to an hour. Tears began falling from my eyes, but it was not "crying", crying, they were just fresh free tears, streaming down my face as I moaned. I sensed the Holy Spirit's presence so strong, I was in awe.

It was at that moment I truly realized what intercessory prayer was all about. I knew without a doubt, that while I was moaning, unable to speak, that the Holy Spirit was telling my Precious Savior everything that I was wanting to say, but couldn't, that had been bottled up over the past two years. I knew that He spoke on my behalf, and asked for my forgiveness of falling into doubt and despair. I knew that He told the Father how much I loved Him, and how much I wanted to serve Him and praise Him and glorify Him. I knew that I had been touched by His mighty hands, an embrace that seemed to last forever. I started praising the Lord and singing and thanking Him for delivering me from that dark time. I remember the Lord telling me not to be concerned about others opinions of my walk, but to just do that which pleases Him and that would be enough.

After I finished, I turned on the flashlight and opened my Bible and I remember flipping through and the Lord telling me to go to Psalms. And this is what He told me:

Psalm 34

Martha, bless the LORD at all times;
Let My praise be continually in your mouth.
Your soul Martha shall make its boast in the LORD;
The humble shall hear of it and be glad.
Oh, magnify the LORD,
And let us exalt His name together.

You sought Me Martha, and I heard you,
And I delivered you from all your fears.
You looked to Me and were radiant,
And your face was not ashamed.
Martha you cried out, and I the LORD heard you,
And saved you out of all your troubles.

My angel encamps all around you because you fear me,
And will deliver you.

Oh, taste and see Martha that the LORD is good;
Blessed are you, for you trust in Me!
Oh, fear the LORD, you His saints!
There is no want to those who fear Him.
The young lions lack and suffer hunger;
But those who seek the Lord shall not lack any good thing.

Come, Martha, listen to me;
I will teach you to fear the Lord.
Who is the man who desires life,
And loves many days, that he may see good?
Keep your tongue from evil,
And your lips from speaking deceit.
Depart from evil and do good;
Seek peace and pursue it.

The eyes of the LORD are on the righteous,
And His ears are open to their cry.
The face of the LORD is against those who do evil,
To cut off the remembrance of them from the earth.

Martha, you cried out, and I the LORD heard,
And I deliver you out of all your troubles.
I am near to you who has a broken heart,
And I will save your contrite spirit.

Many are your afflictions,
But I the LORD deliver you out of them all.
I guard all your bones,
Not one of them is broken.
Evil shall slay the wicked,
And those who hate the righteous shall be condemned.
The LORD redeems the soul of His servants,
And none of those who trust in Him shall be condemned.

I tell you what, I went in that closet a broken pitiful mess, but I came out a broken, but mended, loved child of God…refreshed, renewed, forgiven, and blessed. I then realized that I needed to go through those two years of blah in order to see Him at work. He showed me that although I had severe moments of self-doubt, fear, anxieties, and loneliness, I still chose to pray even when I did not feel like praying, I still read his word when I did not feel like reading, and I trusted in Him even when I thought He was not there. He showed me firsthand, that my faith is not based on feelings; it is based on facts and promises. He is awesome! I praise the Lord for He alone is worthy of all my praise.

Gracious Lord, you are the Magnificent, Awesome, All-Powerful, All-Knowing, Merciful Holy One. My Great Comforter, My Prince of Peace. I thank you for loving me so. I thank you for the healing you brought about in my life. I thank you for the dear ones who will be reading this book someday, who need you as much as I do. Bless them Father, may they sense your peace and your comfort, and your sweet grace you so freely give. Whatever trials they are facing both public and private, be in the midst of them all. May they claim your promises in Psalm 34, and may they find peace and comfort knowing that the Holy Spirit is always in intercessory prayer on our behalf. Thank you Lord Jesus for sweet salvation, thank you for sweet forgiveness, and thank you for the sweet and precious gift you gave on the cross that we may have the abundant life you promised. Bless them, bless me, bless You. In the Precious Name of Jesus,

Amen

Keep the Faith

Father, I need You, I long to feel You near,
Please hold me close, till comfort comes,
Till Your voice I hear.

Speak that I may hear, words of truth from You,
Direct the path before me, that leads me to Your throne.

For Your grace is free to all, who call upon Your name,
Content I'll be, till Jesus comes,
I praise Your Holy Name.

Thank You for peace, Your joy so Divine,
I'll run the race, and keep the faith,
Until Your face I see.

Thank you for peace, Your joy so Divine,
I'll run the race, and keep the faith,
Until Your face I see.

I'll run the race...and keep the faith...until Your face I see.

Chapter 8

Rain Down On Me

There is such power in the name of Jesus, and we have complete use of it. We have the ability to do anything through Christ who strengthens us. It is amazing just how much He loves us and just what all He gave to us. He laid down His life for each and every one of us...the good, the bad, everyone. Christ is not a respecter of persons; He does not just serve the ones that think they are living righteous lives.

He came to this earth in the form of man, lived a perfect and sinless life, suffered and died on a cross, was buried in a borrowed tomb, rose again on the third day - all that we might have eternal life. He ascended to Heaven and God sent a Comforter to us, the Holy Spirit, to dwell in the hearts of every man, woman, and child who called upon His name.

All through the Bible days, children of God suffered through hardships and disappointments. David was constantly being pursued by Saul who wanted to kill him. The same David later pursued a married woman and conceived a child with her. To hide the fact that it was his child he had her husband put on the front line in battle and he was killed. David then married her and made everyone to believe things were as they should be. He thought he had covered his sinful acts. He thought he had it all figured out, but God knew fully everything that took place, and as punishment for his sin, God cursed the child she bore and the baby died.

Then there was Paul who had spent his whole life persecuting Christians and took joy in it. He plotted to have them all destroyed in some form or fashion. But on the road to Damascus he came face to face with God, and he repented of his sins and began serving Christ. However, as a Christian, he still suffered. He had been imprisoned for preaching the gospel.

Another one of God's children was Abraham, he and his wife struggled with conception. They wanted a child, but to no avail. When they were old the Lord blessed them with a child. That very child would become the sacrifice that God wanted Abraham to give on the altar. Abraham was faithful and got as far as raising the knife to slay him, when God provided a ram in the thicket for Abraham to give as a burnt offering to the Lord.

These are not just three stories told in the Bible of men with hardships and disappointments, there are many, many more. The unique thing about each one of these men is that no matter what the bleak circumstances were, they trusted God. They knew the power of calling on the Lord. They knew that no matter what sins they had committed, or what valleys they experienced, or what trials they would have to endure, the power of the Holy Spirit would enable them to rise above their circumstances.

Scripture tells us:

> *"But you shall receive power when the Holy Spirit has come upon you; and you shall be witnesses to Me in Jerusalem, and in all Judea and Samaria, and to the end of the earth."*
> *Acts 1:8*

The Lord gives us the power to overcome any situation we face. He also empowers us to do the things He would have us do. He never leaves us on our own. If we just seek Him and trust in Him, we will survive any storm that comes our way. Satan is always at work. And he is busy thinking of ways to get us all stirred up. We need to stay prayed up and put our armor on daily to protect us from satan and his evil schemes.

> *"Be sober; be vigilant; because your adversary the devil walks about like a roaring lion, seeking whom he may devour."*
> *1Peter 5:8*

The more satan can make us believe we are worthless, the less we can be used by God. Trials and hard times do not always result from sin, sometimes satan asks to sift us, to see what we are made of. He wants to see if we truly love the Lord and are faithful to Him. He wants to trip us up in our walk so that we will not draw others to Christ. The more on fire we are for the Lord, the more satanic attacks we will suffer. But God equips us all through His word and gives us what we need to protect ourselves. I do not like satanic attacks, yet I know they will come. For I know that when satan is messing with me, I have him worried. The more he stays stirred, the more I am doing for the kingdom of God. So I try to always put on my spiritual armor and stay in constant communication with the Lord.

It is difficult at times to stay focused on Christ, for so many things of this world tempt us. And it is often difficult to see God's hand in our lives when we are faced with great turmoil. But that is when we need to rely on His promises. His promises that He will never leave us or forsake us (Hebrews 13:5); or greater is He that is in us, than he that is in the world (1 John 4:4); or my God shall supply all my need (Philippians 4:19). When we recognize an attack from satan, God's Word tells us:

"Therefore submit to God. Resist the devil and he will flee from you. Draw near to God and He will draw near to you. Cleanse your hands, you sinners; and purify your hearts, you double-minded. Lament and mourn and weep! Let your laughter be turned to mourning and your joy to gloom. Humble yourselves in the sight of the Lord, and He will lift you up."
James 4:7-10, NKJV

If we humble ourselves and put Christ first, He will lift us up. That is a wonderful promise that Christ gives us. He tells us it is as simple as that. Resist satan, rebuke him in the name of Jesus and he will flee. That is awesome! With the mere mention of Jesus' name, satan disappears. He cannot be in the same place as Christ.

So when negative thoughts are consuming your mind, trials and tribulations are on every corner, and the deceiver is trying to convince you that you are worthless…do not become a captive of his. Ask Christ to bind up the enemy, and things become clearer. You will start to see that the trial you are going through is meant to draw you closer to the Lord, not destroy you. Life will not seem so bleak.

Pray, pray, pray, and ask the Holy Spirit to rain down on you and fill you with His peace. Read and pray over Ephesians 6, and put on the full armor of God that you may be able to withstand the wiles of the devil. God is good.

Rain Down On Me

Let me learn, let me live,
by the promises of Your holy word.
Resting sure and steadfast, in Your love forevermore.
I'll confess, not distress, over trials in my life.
I'll trust and never doubt, that You will work it out.
I'll seek and I'll find, my strength in You.
Holy Spirit, rain down on me.

Bind up satan, tie him tight, keep him far, far from me.
Let me not give in, to his captivity.
I'll hold to Your word and believe with all my heart,
That I'm fearfully, wonderfully made.

Let me grow, let me share,
of the gift that You gave to me.
Long ago on a hill,
where You died to set my sinful soul free.
I will tell of Your love, of salvation full and free.
About Your saving grace, and what it did for me.
How to trust and never doubt, that You'll work it out.
Holy Spirit, rain down on me.

Bind up satan, tie him tight, keep him far, far from me.
Let me not give in, to his captivity.
I'll hold to Your word and believe with all my heart,
That I'm fearfully, wonderfully made.

By the Maker of my life, the Lover of my soul,
The Beginning and The End, the One who always knows.
The Apple of my eye, my Bright and Morning Star,
My Comforter, my Savior, and my Friend.

Bind up satan, tie him tight, keep him far, far from me.
Let me not give in, to his captivity.
I'll hold to Your word and believe with all my heart,
That I'm fearfully, wonderfully made.

Chapter 9

Greater Still

    Self…what a word. Outside of satan, we can be our own worst enemy. So often I have allowed *self* to get in the way of my walk with the Lord. I have been guilty of being so called, *"righteous"*. I believed that I was doing everything right that God would have me do. Not meaning I think that I am better than anyone else, but righteous in the sense that I knew exactly what to do to make the Lord happy. I had myself convinced that if I read my Bible so much, or prayed just right, or did enough for other people, that I would somehow win God's favor. I had the wrong idea. I had somewhere missed the mark, and misunderstood God in a major way.

    I was saved, I had head knowledge of God, and it worked for awhile. It took me several years of being a so-called "Christian", for me to realize my need to have a heart knowledge of Christ. I had to internalize exactly what it meant to be a child of God. That moment did not come until after I had my first child. It was then that I realized what God had done for me. He gave his one and only Son to die for me. How could he possibly do that?

There is no way I could willingly give my child's life for another person, yet He did. I then began to realize the grace of God. I realized that I never would be able to read my Bible enough, pray enough, or do enough, to earn God's favor. I learned I already was in His favor on the cross. That He freely gave all for me, and for you.

It did not all happen at one time. I was a Christian, but when I read scripture, I just did understand it. So I depended on preachers, and other people to be my God, so I received lots of opinions of God, good and bad. But after having a child of my own, I realized the magnitude of the gift He gave, and it planted a hunger in me to know God more. I started reading the word in a new way. I started asking God to teach me more about Him through His word. It was then that I started learning for myself, how compassionate and loving and forgiving God is. I started learning that He did not care how much I read the Bible; He cared about how much I applied what I *did* read to my life. He did not care how much I prayed, He cared about the attitude in which I prayed, and He did not care how much I did for others, He cared about how much I did for others in the name of Christ.

I can remember realizing the grace that He gave so freely. I can remember being in awe and the feeling of unworthiness that rushed over me. I deserved death on the cross, but He took my place. I starting reading the Word asking God to show me why…why, He loved me so? I remember literally asking Him to give me the eyes I needed to see the answers that I was looking for in the word. I can remember the first passages that seemed to leap off the page at me.

James 1:2-5, NKJV:

> *"My brethren, count it all joy when you fall into various trials, knowing that the testing of your faith produces patience. But let patience have its perfect work, that you may be perfect and complete, lacking nothing. If any of you lacks wisdom, let him ask of God, who gives to all liberally and without reproach, and it will be given unto him."*

Let me tell you, I was excited. I thought it is true. I asked God to give me eyes to see, and He did. I told myself, that's me. I want to be perfect and complete, lacking nothing. I was so excited. I went on to Matthew to read about not worrying about tomorrow. The words spoke to my heart and I was on a spiritual high. I prayed and asked God to enlighten me more and he did. Then eventually, months down the road, I was praying and I could not see God working in my life, and I started doubting that He was even listening to me. I picked up reading in James 1:6, kind of where I left off.

> *"But let him ask in faith, with no doubting, he who doubts is like a wave of the sea driven and tossed by the wind. For let not that man suppose that he will receive anything from the Lord; he is a double-minded man, unstable in his ways."*
> *James 1:6-7*

OOPS, that was me too. I realized that I had been praying, not really expecting God to answer my prayers. It all went back to that unworthiness attitude. Why would God want to answer my prayers? I'm not good enough to have my prayers answered. It was in that passage that God spoke to my heart, saying: "Hey, just ask me anything according to My will and believe it, and it will come to pass."

I began to see that I could not just pull scripture out when it was convenient for me. I had to pursue my walk with the Lord on a regular basis. I started learning that there were more promises He had for me, but I had to search them out on my own in Scripture. No one could do it for me; I had to find out for myself.

I have fallen in love with God over and over again. I so long for His return. I have noticed that when I start finding myself discontented with church; the preacher's message, how a program is running, or even how other people are doing their jobs; that I have taken my eyes off of Christ and started looking to other people to satisfy me. And that is not possible. People are going to let you down. No one can walk a perfect life 24 hours a day. You can follow the so-called, best Christian around daylight until dark, and they will let you down.

Usually when we start finding fault in others, we can almost pinpoint where the discontentment comes from…our relationship with the Lord is suffering. Maybe we become busy with jobs, kids, hobbies, church, and get caught up in the rush and leave God out of the picture. He will eventually get our attention. We need to never put someone in a place that Christ never intended for him or her to be. He is the only Perfect One; He is the only one who can do it right.

Some days I find myself yearning for Christ to come back in all His glory. I get so discouraged at the heartaches and strife that seem to permeate our world. Yet, I know that if He was to come at this very moment, I would not have done all that He has called me to do, and there is so much more I want to do. I allow fear to keep me from always sharing the gospel with others. And I want to get past that. I could write you a note all day long, telling you about the Lord and how to know Him in a personal way, but I freeze up when talking to someone in person. I want to get over that before He comes back.

Greater still, I long to see His face. I long to bask in the presence of God Almighty, and sing and praise Him with arms outstretched, singing as loud as possible, shouting His glory for all to hear. I want to praise Him with no fear of the thoughts of the person sitting next to me. I long to ask questions, to see loved ones, to learn from Him firsthand. I long to see that city; I long to be with the Lord.

Greater Still

*If I never see tomorrow, if I have no more yesterdays.
If I never see today again, I know where I'll be.
I'll be in Heaven with my Savior,
I'll walk down the streets of gold,
I'll touch the pearly gates of Heaven's portals,
Greater still, I'll see His face.*

*I long to see that city, that I've heard of for so long,
I long to see the crystal sea, jasper walls,
and jewels so rare,
Greater still, I long to see His face.*

*The One who first loved me, the One who died for me,
The One who has my heart completely,
The One who saved my soul from hell.*

*So if you never see tomorrow,
if you have no more yesterdays,
If you never see today again, do you know where you'll be?
Will you be in Heaven with the Savior?
Will you walk down the streets of gold?
Will you touch the pearly gates of Heaven's portals?
Or in hell, will your eyes behold?*

*If the question is unanswered,
if your future you don't know.
Call on Him in your heart, and welcome His saving grace,
And His mercy He will bestow.*

*And we'll be in Heaven with our Savior,
We'll walk down the streets of gold,
We'll touch the pearly gates of Heaven's portals,
Greater still, we'll see His face.*

*We'll touch the pearly gates of heaven's portals, greater
still, we'll see His face.*

Chapter 10

Fasting

As I have been writing this book over the past several months, the Lord has brought to my attention many things that I needed to work on in my relationship to Him and others. I have come to a point in my life where I thought I was of no use to the Lord. I have allowed fear and pride get in the way of what God has called me to do. And even though I do not exactly know what that call is at this moment, I realize that I need to find out.

The Lord has brought fasting to my mind many, many times. I have fasted some in the past, a handful of one-day fasts. But He has been wooing me for a while and I have pretty much ignored His prompting. So last week I surrendered to His prompting and began praying to fast. Some friends and I have started preparing to be ready to fast this coming weekend, which happens to be Halloween. I sensed the Lord's leading me to fast for three days. I am not sure why three days, but I am willing to do it in His strength.

I have heard said that you should never tell others when you are fasting. But I believe it is okay to share it as part of a testimony to others in encouraging them to learn the discipline of fasting. I do not claim to have that discipline. Each time I fast it is by trial and error. But, regardless of my technique, be it right or wrong, the Lord has shown me wonderful things through fasting. I am by no means experienced in the area of fasting, but I am looking forward to wonderful things taking place this weekend.

Fasting does not always mean doing totally without food or drink. Fasting is sacrificing something that is a luxury, or a stronghold in your life. For the person who loves watching television, their fast might be doing without television for a day, an afternoon, a particular program, etc. For someone who loves eating out, their fast might be staying in and eating for a month. Each person is unique and each person has something that is a sacrifice to give up. No two are alike.

When we fast we need to ask the Lord what He would have us give up for the fast. We should always pray and seek God's leadership. If your desire is to fast, it is not because you thought of it first. The Lord prompts people to fast. If you want to fast, start asking the Lord about it. Father, do you want me to fast? How long should I fast? What should I give up? How do I do it and when should I start? Just as I said earlier in the book, communication is the key. Ask for His direction. And listen to His voice. We need to seek forgiveness for any sin in our life, known or unknown and repent. Truly lay aside every hurt, mishap, fear, or excuse and seek His guidance. Try not to be in a rush, listen patiently for His reply, in His time.

So with all this said, I am going to do something that probably goes against all reason. I want to invite you to join me. As I prepare this week for the fast, you all can be my accountability partners. I have never done anything like this, but I just want you to see first hand, how precious this time can be. This is new territory for me.. I have never written a book, I have never shared my journals in detail, I have never completed a three day fast, I have never prepared for a three day fast, I have never opened my thought life up for others to see. So if you are experienced in fasting, praise the Lord for you, pray for me. If you are new to fasting, then praise the Lord for you, pray for me. If you are thinking I'm a nut, then praise the Lord for you, you are probably right. So let's go. I can't wait to see how it all comes about.

Monday, Oct.25

Today as I sought the Lord, He reminded me once again of an area I needed to seek forgiveness from Jay. The Lord already had forgiven me for it, but He wanted me to talk to Jay about it. He told me two weeks ago to talk to Jay, but I kept putting it off. Tonight I finally heeded his instructions. It was so good. We had a great talk and Jay was so kind and compassionate to me. One thing at a time God is purifying me and getting me ready to hear from Him this weekend. I have started tapering off on my meals, eating fish and vegetables. Tomorrow will be pretty light, working towards soup on Wednesday and Thursday. We are looking to start our fast Thursday night at 6:00pm. I sense the Lord leading me to a complete fast, water only. I have never done this before, but I know He will help me do it. I am so excited to see the Lord's movement through this time. Got to go to bed, it is late.

Tuesday, Oct. 26

Today has been a pretty good day; I started out first thing this morning by putting on the armor of God. I've been praying for the Lord to show me what to do next. I didn't get to spend as much time in prayer as I should today, but nonetheless, this fast has been on my mind. Oatmeal with a slice of wheat toast for breakfast. A salad at lunch with grilled chicken, walnuts, apples, and raisins on it. (Delicious!) Suppertime I had a spoonful of this and that at a covered dish supper at the church for Pastor Appreciation month. My last splurge for the week. So it is now bedtime and I am about to listen to some worship music and start my prayer time. So goodnight, sleep tight, don't let the bedbugs bite, and all that good stuff.

Wednesday, Oct. 27

Another day closer. Today has been a fairly nice day. No breakfast today, no reason, other than laziness. Read a little while, then cleaned house. By 11:00am, I realized I never did eat breakfast. So I fixed a bowl of soup and a slice of wheat bread. And for supper, I ate out with my sister-in-law. I had soup, salad, and some chicken nachos. Nachos weren't necessarily on my list of things I planned to eat, but they were good anyhow. This afternoon I started realizing that I had no breakfast this morning, my stomach was talking to me a bit. Then I started thinking, gee, if missing breakfast makes me feel this way, how will I make it three days? Then almost instantly, the Lord reassured me that I could, and I recognized satan's attempts to make me think I couldn't participate in a fast. Satan get thee behind me. I am so excited. I haven't even started the actual fast itself, yet God is already moving in small ways. Today he brought some information to light, that I had asked Him about. I can see Him working in different areas of my life. Thank you Jesus.

Thursday, Oct. 28

    Today was nice. I kind of took it easy. The kids and I went and visited a friend who lives at the beach. I just sat and relaxed on her porch and just worshipped the Lord and the beauty of His creation looking out over the ocean. Praise the Lord for His marvelous creation. Bagel and cream cheese with a banana for breakfast today. Chinese food for lunch and a grilled chicken sandwich and potatoes for supper and a homemade fruit smoothie. Okay this is it for a few days. I started getting a little antsy earlier, but I just prayed my way through it and feel much better now. I am so looking forward to this time of refreshment and renewal from the Lord. Heading for bed now, 5am will be coming early. Three or four of us will be meeting at the church in the morning for prayer and worship, all expecting great things. Goodnight.

Friday, Oct. 29 – Day one of fast.

    This morning we met at the church at 5:30am to pray for and with each other, and to lift up our petitions and fasts to the Father. We had a very nice time in prayer. As the day went on I thought of the Lord often. I prayed off and on all day. However, I didn't get to spend any alone time with the Father. I was on the go and kids with me all day. I am looking forward to some quiet time alone tomorrow. Tonight I have got to spend some time with the Father. I have hunger pains off and on, but I have recited the Lord's Prayer through some, and pray my own prayers through the others. The Lord has been revealing to me how much emphasis I have put on food. I have been realizing that all that I do or don't do is a matter of choices. I am very tired and am going to sleep. I am looking forward to tomorrow and looking forward to the Lord's movement. Praise God.

Saturday, Oct. 30, Day 2 of fast

    I awoke and went to the church at 5:30am and met the others for prayer. We had a very intense prayer time for healing over a dear person. This person has been battling severe depression, which has been diagnosed as bipolar. We first listened to some worship music then went into prayer. Whenever the first lady started praying, I felt the presence of the Holy Spirit so strong around us. Glory bumps went from the back of my neck down to my heels. I was so totally engrossed in her prayer, that when it was my turn to pray, I was speechless. It was a precious time to me. I am thankful for that prayer time. Later on today around 1:30pm, I sensed the Lord telling me that I needed to end my fast. I told Him that I was doing fine, I wasn't even really that hungry, and that I was fine to keep going. But He made it clear to me that it was over. So I ended the fast. When I later checked my email, my niece who lives in Arkansas, had sent me a very sweet encouraging note. She wrote: *I went and bought Joyce Meyer's book today called "Straight Talk". I have not started reading it yet though, but let me flip through the pages and see what I can find for you. Try this. I don't know what the situation is that you are dealing with but maybe this will help...*

> *We don't always have to do some great spiritual thing. Actually some of the things we don't think are really spiritual are more important to God than the things we think are so great.*
>   --Joyce Meyer, Straight Talk

I was so blessed by these words. I felt a little weird stopping the fast that I had planned to do longer, and thought, *"Lord, why did you want me to stop?"* But these words that she sent me were perfect. He spoke to my heart through her email. He told me that a three-day fast wasn't necessarily what he wanted me to do, although it is a great spiritual thing. He made me realize that the prayer and preparation for the fast meant just as much to Him as the fast itself. That I was obedient to listen to Him was enough. Now, know that my niece lives in Arkansas, and I have not talked to her in three weeks. She was replying to an email that I had sent her a week before. She had no clue that I was fasting or that I had just ended a fast. God is so good. He knew that I needed confirmation and He gave it. This has been an awesome day. I got to spend much time with the Lord this morning, although I was mostly quiet, I just rested in Him. Thank you Lord Jesus.

October 31, Day 3

Although I stopped fasting yesterday, the girls and I met this morning for prayer. The dear friend whom we had prayed for who is suffering from bipolar depression, came with us to our prayer time at 5:30am. I was so excited she decided to come. One of the ladies brought some oil. So we all gathered around her and anointed her with oil and laid hands on her as we prayed. This was such a beautiful time. I could sense the Lord near and I knew without a shadow of a doubt that God was using this weekend and this fast in a mighty way. I do not know what all will come from this weekend, but it has been a blessing to my heart. We have taken turns being broken before the Lord, and He is faithful and just to take our burdens and carry our load. Praise the Lord for His goodness and mercy. This has been such a delightful weekend. Two of the women sensed the Lord's deliverance from some burdens they were carrying. If nothing else this weekend five women grew a lot closer to the Lord. I love you Lord. You are My Strength and My Redeemer.

Fasting is a discipline that you learn about more and more as you try it. I may not do things as well as others when it comes to fasting, but I am learning as God teaches me more about His ways. I have had a delightful past three days. The Lord has given me some answers, but not all. But what He has given me is a greater love and respect for Him. Each day that brings me closer to Him, is a day well spent.

Pray and ask God about fasting. It is a wonderful experience. There does not have to be fireworks and hoopla; you just need a humble heart, some quiet time, and a willingness to hear from God. I encourage you to start reading different books on fasting and look in the Bible itself for those people who fasted and why they fasted. You may be surprised at what you find.

As I woke up today,
Thankful for time well spent.
I became excited in His glory,
And thanked Him for all He meant.
Never has there been a time,
When I've come before His throne.
That His arms weren't open and outstretched,
That His glory wasn't shown.
I thank you Father, For your mercies great.
Your grace sufficient still.
I thank you for your loving touch,
That keeps me in your will.

Chapter 11

Peace Be Still

Peace is such a wonderful thing. The calmness after a hurricane blows through, the sweet sleep of a newborn baby, or the stillness of the night after most of the world is in bed. But no matter what we call peace, there is nothing like the peace of God that surpasses all understanding. God is true to His word. He is in control of all things and though at times it is hard to be still and let Him be in control, He can speak peace into the most difficult circumstances. You can be in the most horrific circumstance but God has the power to bring His peace to the situation.

Prayer has become my peace. When I am consumed with doubts, fears, anxieties, and frustration, I have become fully reliant on God and His insurmountable peace. So many times He has been there when it seemed no one else was around. Prayer is essential to survive the ups and downs of this life. When we open ourselves up to prayer, we open ourselves up to the riches He has stored up for us. When I speak of riches, I do not mean monetary things. The riches of His glory are those of love, joy, peace, long-suffering, kindness, goodness, gentleness, and self-control. He equips us with all we need to weather the havoc that life at times throws at us.

A couple of years ago, we were struggling financially. My husband's work had slowed and we were behind on bills. There was not much peace going on in my mind. I was consumed with fear. I counted up and I had figured to the best of my ability that we needed $1500.00 to *catch* us up on some seriously past due bills, and to pay some current bills. I was lying in bed crying and telling my husband…What are we going to do? We talked and neither knew the answer. He was drifting off to sleep, (How do men do that?) and I was on alert, doing my part to lay there and worry (which yes, is sinning). Finally, around 11:00 p.m., I told my husband that I was going to go watch the 700 Club on television.

Often times while praying, Pat Robertson and his staff will speak words of knowledge over people that God brings to their heart and minds. Several years ago, I was healed through prayer as I was praying with them. I had surgery on my neck a couple of months prior to this particular night. I still was having complications during healing with tingling and burning sensations where my incision had been, as well as, occasional stabbing pains. As they were praying aloud, I was praying and telling the Father that I was in need of healing on my neck. I was tired of the pain and was in intense prayer as they were praying. As I finished my words, I heard Pat speak as he was praying, "There is a woman who is suffering from pain from neck surgery. Her incision is having trouble healing, stabbing pains and such. Know that God is healing you right now." My concentration was broken and I told the Lord, "Thank You, I claim that promise." Goosebumps seemed to reach from head to toe. From that night forward, I no longer suffered from pain. I know without a doubt I was healed that night.

So here again I found myself watching the 700 Club. When it came time for them to pray, I started praying at the same time, telling the Father that I was scared and that I knew that He could provide the $1500.00 just by speaking it into existence. As I finished praying those words, I heard one of the people on the TV praying and his exact words were: There is a lady praying right now over her finances, it looks to be about $1500.00, your prayer is being answered, have no fear. Let me tell you, a warm tingling sensation went over my entire body. I claimed that promise, I raised my hands in the air and said, *" Father, that is me, I know you are providing."* I had a peace come over my mind and heart that I could not even begin to explain. I started giggling and praising the Father. I probably looked like a nut if anyone was watching, but I was having me a time in the Lord.

I went to bed and woke Jay out of a good sleep at about 12:00 a.m. This was about the way the conversation went:

Me: Jay, you awake? (granted I am laughing the entire time I am trying to talk to him.)
Jay: Uh huh! (still obviously asleep)
Me: I just wanted to tell you to go to sleep and don't worry, God is giving us $1500.00. (He's still not completely alert)
Jay: Uhh? (Starting to stir)
Me: I'm okay Jay, I'm not upset anymore, God just gave me a word of knowledge and He is going to give us the $1500.00, don't really know when, but it is coming. (Giggling and crying all at the same time)

Jay: Okay honey, go to sleep. (Not really taking it all in, but probably glad he heard I was going to sleep)

    I went on to sleep and the next morning he vaguely remembered me talking to him. I told him once again what took place and he said, okay. He has learned me well enough by now to not question, just nod in agreement like he gets me. That is what I love the most about Jay; he just lets me be me, crazy and all. Anyhow this took place on a Tuesday or Wednesday. The job he was working on was not going to be finished and we knew no paycheck was coming that week. On Friday, a man who owed him from a job about 6 months prior to that day paid him $700, unexpectedly. I was so excited. Jay said, "yeah, but that's not $1500.00". I said, "I know… but it's coming". I knew because of the peace the Lord had given me from the few nights prior to the money. On Tuesday they completed the job and they received more than expected due to some returned supplies. When he received his part it was exactly $800.00. In less than a week, God had given us the $1500.00 we needed, in ways that could not have been thought of. It was a very exciting time for Jay and me both. Still to this day, I do not think he would ever mind if I wake him up in the middle of the night, haha.

    Believe me there have been many nights that I pray for things that do not seem to get answered the way I would want them to. But God is so cool to knock my socks off at times. There has been many a time that no money came, but the peace was there. And guess what, we survived the crisis at the time.

God is always faithful to remind me of His promises in His word. It is so important that we read and memorize God's word and hide it in our hearts. I often times go get my Bible and say, "Lord, I need a promise" and I will open my Bible and there it will be. Or he will bring to my mind a verse of scripture to bring me peace and comfort. If we seek Him, He will meet us right where we are. All we need to do is slip away and pray. He'll do the rest.

Peace Be Still

When trials of this life, seem tough and hard to bear,
And an answer is no where in sight.
Just slip away and pray, and call with all you have,
Then step back and see Him in all His might.

Peace be still, when the storms are raging all around.
Peace be still, when answers are few.
His grace is the way, to master any storm
Just relax and say, peace be still.
The sun'll come up in the morn.

So today was not so good, the office was much too stressful,
And the troubles were on every hand.
Just slip away and pray, and call with all you have,
Then step back and see Him in all His might.

Peace be still, when the storms are raging all around.
Peace be still, when answers are few.
His grace is the way, to master any storm
Just relax and say, peace be still.
The sun'll come up in the morn.

I will not grow weary, in this race that I must run,
I'll not give in to doubt and despair,
I trust in Him, the Meeter of my needs,
As I slip away and pray, and call with all I have.

Peace be still, when the storms are raging all around.
Peace be still, when answers are few.
His grace is the way, to master any storm
Just relax and say, peace be still.
The sun'll come up in the morn.

Peace be still... the sun'll come up in the morn.

Chapter 12

Once Again

      Here I am once again. I know that it would seem I just finished the previous chapter and started a new one. However, it has been several months since I have even picked up this book to start writing again. I have been going through some really trying times. Every time I would think to pick up the book, something else took its place. I have been exhausted and down. Satan has been on the rampage in my thoughts, my attitude, my marriage, my church, and more. I knew opposition would come as I strive to write as God would lead me, I just was not expecting it to be so soon.

      The whole time I have spent writing this book, the Lord has told me what to write. I have not had to sit and think, "What do I write now?" It just came to me and I wrote it. However, the past few months I have struggled. Nothing comes to mind, just blank. In fact, I questioned whether or not to even try to finish it. I became really discouraged and on the verge of losing hope, and did not feel as though I needed to be writing a book. I have come to realize that I have been walking in my own strength, instead of Christ's strength.

I have been missing church some, and had found myself backing away from things like…lunches with friends, Sunday School, singing, and finding discontentment in nearly every area of my life, including my church. Pity party central! I could sense myself slipping further away from God, yet I was content in doing so. My heart seemed to be hardened.

I can not really pinpoint exactly when this all started taking place, but I know how. I started letting circumstances rule my thoughts. I had backed off of my prayer time, studying my Bible and most importantly my quiet time with the Lord. Everything that I have written about seemed to be taking place in my life once again. How do I do that so well? I long to draw closer to God, yet I seem to walk the opposite direction from Him.

I had been somewhat avoiding the preacher and his sermons, for I was afraid he might say something that I needed to hear, avoiding correction at all costs. I have even contemplated leaving the only church home I have ever had, which has been my home for 15 years now. What? Martha? Are you nuts? There have been a lot of changes taking place in my life here lately as well as at church. Our church body is growing at a drastic pace…which should be a big "Praisalujah!" However, it seems chaotic. Things that have always been done one way are being done another way now. People who once said nothing are saying something now. People who once were stagnant in the church are becoming on fire for the Lord. It all sounds good and it is, however, when things are chaotic in my life, my house, my work, my kids, my marriage, my everything;

my church has always been unchanging. It was my comfort, my safety net. When life seemed out of control I could run to church and things and people were there…same as always. That whole "CONTROL" issue. I can not control what takes place there any more than I can control what takes place in my life. I have been running and losing hope and trying to find where I can go. Do not get me wrong, this is a beautiful thing taking place at our church. I sense God moving in a mighty way and I see revival breaking out.

    What I see and what makes me a little nervous is…what is God about to ask me to do? I have been active in church many years, but I have been discontented here lately. Discontentment is usually a result of disobedience. Which in turn means, somewhere I am missing the mark. Where am I supposed to be in my walk with the Lord? This is all that has been running through my mind over the past few months. That was until this morning. I purposely skipped Sunday school, did not "feel" like going, half-heartedly went to worship service, trying to muster the ability to sing and act as though I were content. I closed my eyes through the song and prayed and asked God's forgiveness and asked Him to speak to my heart and show me what I need to do to get past this feeling of emptiness I was experiencing.

    The preacher started delivering his sermon and his question to us all was…How are you handling circumstances in your life? Are you living life large or is life living larger than you? He then made a statement that definitely caught my attention. He said, "I can see some of you ready to leave the church, I can tell by your eyes you want to leave." He had my number. Isn't it amazing how

God can speak right through preachers directly into our realm of thinking? He went on to say that we needed to pray to God and ask Him to help us to do more and be more for God and ask Him to move our boundary lines in order to live above our circumstances. He referenced scripture to 1 Chronicles 4:10;

> *"And Jabez called on the God of Israel saying, "Oh, that you would bless me indeed, and enlarge my territory, that Your hand would be with me, and that You would keep me from evil, that I may not cause pain."*

Once again, I realized that I had taken my eyes off Christ, I quit reading His word as I should, I quit trying to apply scripture to my life, I had just quit. I allowed the circumstances in my life to cloud my judgment. I guess why I am sharing this with you all is to show you that it is just that easy, that easy to lose sight of the goal before us. When we stop praying and stop reading, stop asking God daily for the grace to get through it, we lose touch and start drifting away from Him. He never leaves us nor forsakes us. It is I who walked away, not Christ.

I truly believe that God is preparing me to step outside the boundaries that I have placed on Him. With God all things are possible... I am *so* starting to get that into my head. I have no idea where this book is going or where it will be taking me, but I am certain that God knows. I am excited for this is the first time in my life that I am almost certain that I am living the purpose He has for me. I am slowly but surely letting go of the reins and allowing God to carry me, that I may live larger than life and enjoy the abundant life found only in Him.

I believe the evil one has been planting opposition in front of me to see what I am made of and if I truly trust Christ. I know on some days I wanted to believe satan's lies, but I see the liar first and foremost, and I reclaim the victory. I can do all things through Christ who strengthens me.

Gracious Father,

Please forgive me for my negativity, for my complaining and grumbling. Thank you for loving me, thank you for showing me the error of my ways, thank you for wooing me and drawing me back into fellowship with you. I pray Father God, that you would bless me indeed, and enlarge my territory, that Your hand would be with me, and that You would keep me from evil, that I may not cause pain. Give me strength, forgive me of my sins. You are awesome Oh Lord. You are Holy and worthy of all praise and adoration. Forgive me for walking away, and thank you for leading me back to you. I give You glory and honor and praise. In Christ' precious name, Amen

Once Again

Where do I go, when all hope seems drear?
And where do I go, when I'm succumbed by fear?

I'll run to the Lord, I'll rest in Him, and His word.
I'll wait on the Lord, for His mercy endures.
He tells me, to trust in Him, And so I shall...once again.

Where do I go, when all hope seems drear?
And where do I go, when I'm succumbed by fear?

I've waded in the waters of sin, I've chosen my own path,
I've felt the chords of doubt, strangled by their wrath.
Yet he hears my mercy cries,
He stands waiting to take the reins.
He forgives me for my selfish plight,
and renews my heart...once again.

Oh, where do I go, when all hope seems drear?
And where do I go, when I'm succumbed by fear?

I'll run to the Lord, I'll rest in Him, and His word.
I'll wait on the Lord, for His mercy endures.
He tells me, to trust in Him, and so I shall...once again.

So brother, where do you go, when all hope seems drear?
And where will you go, when you're succumbed by fear?

Run to the man with outstretched arms,
there's safety in that place.
He's waiting at your hearts door, listening for your knock.
All hope is in Him, when we seek His face.

Let us go, to the Lord, where no hope is drear,
Let's go, to the Lord,
where we won't be succumbed by fear.
For there we'll find mercy...once again.

Chapter 13

Praise the Lord, Amen

Prayer is such a privilege, that we often take for granted. Just the freedom to go to God with our every thought; be it a burden, a request, praise, or just to talk with Him and listen to Him speak and rest in Him. Prayer is such a precious time to just praise the Father and worship Him, whether individually or corporately.

When I am alone and praying I often times just call Him by His different names. When I am praying for healing, I pray to Jehovah-Rapha, the Lord who heals. Maybe I will pray to Jehovah-Jireh, the Lord who provides. I am not saying that there is more than one God. I am saying that God has several names, all throughout Scripture. Each name reflects a different relationship to us. For example, I am Martha, yet I have other names, according to my relationship to that person. I am a mother to my kids, a sister to my siblings, my mother's daughter, my husband's wife, my nieces' and nephews' aunt, and so on. I have a different relationship with each one and I respond to each one differently. I am still one person, but I have many names or titles I should say.

How I would respond to my husband who is my best friend and lover would be different than how I respond to my children. That is the way I see Christ responding to us.

There are several books out there that explain the different names of God. I could never begin to name them all, however, in prayer I have an opportunity to pray to any name I choose. My Strength, My Redeemer, Gracious Lord, Heavenly Father, Magnificent Creator, Prince of Peace, Mighty God, Awesome Lord, King of Kings, Lord of Lords, Jehovah-Jireh, Jehovah-Rapha, Yahweh, El-Shaddai, Adonai, numerous names.

The freedom to praise Him and pray to Him has over time become hindered. We have gotten away from praying long and with great fervency, to rushing through due to time barriers we put on ourselves. Or maybe some have never been there; maybe you have never experienced fervent prayer. The kind of prayer that brings tears, the kind of prayer that may keep you on your knees so long that you can not feel your toes anymore. Maybe it is time we did. We all fall short of the glory of God, we all sin, we all struggle in our faith at some time or another, and no one is perfect. Not one person is the perfect pray-*er*, no one does it all right or all wrong. Each one of our walks with the Lord is different, but our goal should be the same…strive to know Him better, to become more like Him each and every day He gives us until He calls us home. We do that by praying.

I attended a meeting on prayer; rather it was about building praying churches. The speaker shared how we as Christians tend to constantly lift up prayer needs, such as healing, physical needs, finances, etc., but often times forget to give God the praise and adoration due Him. I am guilty of such, I sometimes get in the rut of, Lord touch this person, Lord heal this person, Lord remove this burden,

Lord this, Lord that, and then I wonder why I am unable to hear Him. I have been so busy telling Him everything I need and want that I fail to be quiet so I can hear Him. But when I am broken and humbled before God in earnest prayer that is when those names begin flowing off my tongue. When I am praising Him the names come with great ease.

This speaker had us each say a name of God that meant something to us. He started by saying "God is..." then went around the room. Different responses were: God is Love, God is Righteousness, God is Faithful, God is Precious, God is Gracious, God is Omnipotent, and more. After about a dozen responses, when we finished, something so incredible happened. A hush came over us, some had tear-filled eyes, others smiling, others eyes closed. In an instant you could feel the presence of the Holy Spirit so strong, with just the mention of His names. The speaker brought to our attention the aura in the room. That was the point that he was trying to make. God inhabits the praises of His people, and recognizing Him by His different names brings Him glory and praise.

As I said earlier in the book, I do not know it all, just the One and All. I long for you to find the time to know this One and All. I long for each and every person that reads this book to find the courage to pray, unhindered and uncontrollable prayers. It is my desire that you find peace and contentment in praying to the Father. I know you will find a satisfaction beyond comparison when you do.

Praying alone is a good thing, but also praying corporately is a much needed time. There is something about several individuals praying together, standing in agreement over a need or request that does the heart good. Prayer makes things happen for the good always, if we pray according to God's will.

> *"Again I say to you that if two of you agree on earth concerning anything that they ask, it will be done for them by My Father in heaven. For where two or three are gathered in My name, I am there in the midst of them."*
> Matthew 18:19-20, NKJV

What a promise! God is so good. He tells us plainly to meet together in prayer and in agreement, of one mind and of one accord, bringing our petitions to Him and He will meet us there. If we pray and ask for anything according to His divine will, He will give it. Granted you might not see a new Mercedes in your driveway, however, if it is God's will for you to have one you better get your fancy driving shoes on. When we start praying for God's will in a situation we open up the opportunity for God to work in and through our prayers. If we just give Him lip service and make deals, He will not heed our prayers. We will most probably walk away thinking that He did not hear us or does not care. When we start praying God's will, our attitudes and desires start to change. We no longer want everything; we begin wanting what God wants us to have.

Corporate prayer is a beautiful time of refreshment and encouragement. Not only does God show up on the spot and bless us beyond measure, He uses other people's words to encourage us. When my youngest son was 6 months old he had to have emergency surgery. He nearly died and we were very scared and concerned. I prayed fervently for my son on my own at times, but something beautiful took place in my heart when my husband and I prayed together. I saw a grown man completely humbled before God, crying out for mercy for our son, totally broken. It was not many words and at this time I can not even remember the words spoken, but what I do remember is the peace that swept over my heart as he prayed.

A peace that God spoke to my heart that our Father loved our son even more than we did, if that is possible, and that he was in God's loving hands whether He chose to take him or allow him to stay here with us.

    Such peace flooded my soul and I knew that I no longer needed to fear. Don't get me wrong, I wanted God to heal him and keep him here, but I let go and told God, You know better than I, Your will be done. I am glad to say that He answered our prayers and our son is still with us today. I truly believe I would not have felt that sense of peace had we not prayed together. Corporate prayer does not mean there has to be oodles of people, just a group, no matter how big or small coming together to praise the Father, worship Him, adore Him, and ask Him with humbled hearts to move in a mighty way.

> *Gracious Father, Precious Lord, Beautiful Savior,*
>   *Thank you. You are awesome and worthy of all things great. You are All-Knowing and All-Powerful, You are my Prince of Perfect Peace, My Comfort in times of trouble, My Abba Father, My Daddy, and You know my thoughts from afar off. You know when my heart is troubled, You know when I am content, You know me inside and out. Your word tells me that You knew me before time began. You are magnificent. I lift up each one that reads this book and I pray that You would put a burning desire in each and every one of their hearts to know You in a more intimate way. I pray that they would seek Your face in private, as well as in a group of people. There are so many needs daily that we have, but none are greater than our need for You. Your word says that You will supply all our need. I pray your perfect will would be done in each of our lives. I pray that each one of us would discover our true purpose in Your kingdom work.*

I praise You Father, for you alone are worthy. Speak to our hearts, give us ears to hear, eyes to see, and hearts to obey. Blessed be the Lord, God of Israel, who does wondrous things for us. Let the whole earth be filled with Your glory,
In Christ's Holy name,
Amen

Praise the Lord, Amen

Praise is awaiting You, O God.
And to You the vow, shall be done.
O You, who hears prayer, to You all flesh will come.
And He shall live, and daily shall be praised.

Blessed be the Lord, God of Israel,
who only does wondrous things for me,
And blessed be His glorious name, forever.
Let the whole earth be filled, with His glory, Amen.

From the rising of the sun, to it's going down.
The Lord's name's to be praised, Praise the Lord.
It is pleasant and praise is beautiful.
Let everything that has breath, Praise the Lord.

Blessed be the Lord, God of Israel,
Who only does wondrous things for you,
and blessed be His glorious name, forever.
Let the whole earth be filled, with His glory, Amen.

Heal me Lord, and I shall be healed.
Save me, and I shall be saved.
For You are my praise, and forever will I be,
In Your constant care, throughout eternity.

Blessed be the Lord, God of Israel,
Who only does wondrous things for us,
and blessed be His glorious name, forever.
Let the whole earth be filled, with His glory, Amen.

Chapter 14

Go, Therefore

In today's world of reality television, guts and glamour action movies, and the like, our society has become calloused to violence, death, and catastrophe. What you or I take in our hearts is what we value. What we watch on television, listen to on the radio, or discuss with people, infiltrates our hearts and minds. If I watch a movie with people being murdered it does not mean I will go out and murder, but it causes my heart to numb a bit.

I used to watch scary or violent movies and it never really bothered me. I knew that it was not real and that it was just a bunch of actors, make-up and all. Until one night, my husband and I rented a movie about a serial killer. We watched the whole movie and it had its gory moments, and thought how terrible that would be to be stalked by someone or be a victim of him. After the movie ended the words appeared on the screen, "THIS MOVIE WAS BASED ON TRUE EVENTS". It then went on to say where the killer was imprisoned at, and how victim's families were moving on. All of a sudden I felt sick to my stomach. When I realized that yeah, these are actors, but what they are acting out is taking place every day in our society. It is a very real thing. I have not watched movies of that nature since, it hurt my heart. My husband often says that we train the serial killers, murderers, and thieves of the world by instructing them in a movie how to do it and get away with it. Violence, death, and hurting people are part of our world. It is our job as believers in Christ, to share the gospel with a lost and dying world. We need to be about the Lord's business, sharing the gospel with every one we meet.

  I struggle with confrontation, I often times fear the unknown. How will people respond if I ask them about Jesus? Will they knock me in the nose, slam the door in my face, or laugh hysterically at me? What? But God's word says that we are to go out and make disciples of all the nations. God promises that if when we go out to witness to someone who is lost, the Lord our God is with us always. What is there to fear when God is with us? We need to share God's love, He commanded us to do so. We need not fear what others may say or do as a result of hearing the gospel. We plant the seed, God gives the increase. He will do His perfect will if we will just trust in Him. People are not rejecting us; they are rejecting Christ when they turn away from the Truth.

  Before the World Trade Center was attacked, I had never really thought of the Twin Towers or terrorism for that matter. I knew that terrorism existed and was dangerous, but I naively thought that it only happened in other countries. A friend of mine called and told me to turn the news on that the World Trade Center had been hit by a hi-jacked plane. As I watched, trying to fathom what was happening, it showed the second plane crashing into the other tower. It seemed as though I was watching a movie.

I just sat there numb, until I saw people start jumping out of the building, knowing that their peril was death, but chose to die that way instead of burning to death. I went to my knees, crying and unable to breathe, it became very real.

I know God is in control and that He has a plan for everything, but I would be lying if I told you that I did not question His control at that very moment. My heart was burdened, I was stunned and scared. I called out and said, "God have mercy on those people." All I knew to do was pray. I turned the television off, called my kids to me, and we prayed. They did not understand what was happening, but they knew momma was upset and they bowed their heads in prayer with me.

Over the next few weeks, I could see God's hand in all that was said and done. I saw how Christ took such a tragedy and brought people together. People mended relationships, things became clearer, and priorities were put into perspective. He knew His purpose for all the attacks on September 11, 2001. He knew the lives that were taken, He knew the families who suffered great loss, and He knew a country that was in need of God. Through those tragedies people came to know the Lord, a country started praying again, people came together in ways that would not have happened otherwise.

Over time we have started to sink back into the same routine, going about our daily business without giving thought to those around us who might be hurting. We need to be disciples and be discipled. We need to encourage one another in our walk with the Lord. We need to get a good dose of reality and start listening when we talk to people. Listen to what they are saying, what their heart is saying. All of us should be moved to compassion when someone has a need. But, I believe we have become numb to people and to their needs, and fear that we do not know how to help or make a difference. So therefore, we do nothing.

I am not saying that none of us ever help others or pray for them and such, I just mean that if we are not careful we could easily fall into that category.

This morning I visited a church as I was away from home for the weekend. The people were very nice and made me feel welcomed. When it came time for prayer requests different ones raised their hands, mentioning their needs. One little girl, about 7 or 8 years old was sitting on the front row alone with her hand raised. She was at church alone, someone must of have picked her up for church, or family dropped her off. She kept her hand raised the entire time the preacher was calling on the other people who had their hands raised. He did not see her, but she waited patiently. Finally, the pianist got the preacher's attention, and he said, "Yes, young lady, what is your request?" The little girl said, "My uncle's house burned down and he died in it." The preacher said, "Okay, thank you." Then he started praying, never mentioning the little girl, or even acknowledging what she just shared.

Everything in me wanted to go scoop the girl up and take her in the other room and pray with her and see if there was a need she or her family had. But I didn't, I let the fear of what people would think override what God was telling me to do. I am not saying the preacher did not care, I'm just noting that every one of us in that room just listened, with numbed hearts, no action took place. It made me realize that *we do* need to disciple and train one another how to listen to God and respond in love at all costs. God clearly tells us in Matthew 28:19-20, NKJV:

> *"Go therefore and make disciples of all the nations, baptizing them in the name of the Father and of the Son and of the Holy Spirit, teaching them to observe all things that I have commanded you; and lo, I am with you always, even to the end of the age."*

There are so many people in need of a Savior today. We need to be about the business of God. We need to be sharing Jesus to a lost and dying world. We need to start looking into people's eyes when we are talking to them and listen to their hearts.

When someone is in need of prayer, we need to be praying for that need, not just pass over as though it did not exist. So many people in our churches today are hurting, yet no one in the pew next to them is aware. Pride takes over and we do not want to share our problems with someone else. Isn't that ridiculous? We need one another so desperately, yet we can not even ask. And it is not just in churches. There are people all over the world hurting, needing a friend, needing for someone to share Jesus and tell them how He loves them and can help them. They may not even be aware of their need for Jesus. We have become so consumed with the world and trying to get by, that we fail to minister to God's people. This is a me, me, me world. What can I do for me? Not what can I do for someone else today.

Prayer is the cure. I do not say all these things to bring doom and gloom in our minds. I am excited at the work the Lord has before us. I want everyone to get excited. The only way to achieve that is through prayer and reading God's word. We need to actively pray for the needs of those around us and those abroad. We need to be bold and step out in faith knowing that Christ is with us always. Wherever we go, whomever we share with, Christ is with us.

This morning I should have gone to that little girl, I should have prayed with her, I should have comforted her. I should have allowed Christ to use me to minister to her and her family. I should not have let the fear of others opinions cripple me. Forgive me, Father.

The thing is this, had I stepped up and went to the little girl and prayed, everyone else would have joined me. I am certain that there was not a person in there who would not have, but they are in the same boat as I was, fear of going against the ordinary. So let's look at scripture and be encouraged to strive for Christ.

> *"For God has not given us a spirit of fear, but of power and of love and of a sound mind."*
> *2 Timothy 1:7, NKJV*

Let us pray together 2 Timothy 1: 7-12, that we may be bold and serve the Lord unhindered.

> *Gracious Father, Our Savior, Our Strength,*
> *We thank you dear God for the power and love and sound mind You have given us that we wouldn't have a spirit of fear. We will not be ashamed of the testimony of You our Lord, but we will share in the sufferings for the gospel according to Your power God, that has saved us and called us with a holy calling, not according to our works, but according to Your own purpose and grace which Jesus Christ gave us before time began. May we not be ashamed, for we know whom we have believed and have been persuaded that You are able to keep that which You have committed until that day. May we be about doing Your blessed will. May we go therefore, and disciple all the nations, baptizing them in the name of the Father and of the Son and of the Holy Spirit, teaching one another to observe all things that You have commanded, and we know that You will be with us always, even to the end of the age. In Jesus' precious name we pray,*
> *Amen.*

Go, Therefore

Go, therefore, and disciple all the nations.
Go, therefore, and disciple all the nations.
Teach them to obey, everything that He's commanded.
Tell them all about His love.

Have you a heavy heart; is the load to hard to bear?
Do you ever question, that He really even cares?
Do you want all the answers, are you prepared to know?
Then take up your cross and set out on the road.

Go, therefore, and disciple all the nations.
Go, therefore, and disciple all the nations.
Teach them to obey, everything that He's commanded.
Tell them all about His love.

He'll meet you where you're at; He'll pick up your load.
He'll comfort and guide you, as you onward go.
Your cup will runneth over,
you'll love Him more and more.
When you take up your cross, and set out on the road.

Go, therefore, and disciple all the nations.
Go, therefore, and disciple all the nations.
Teach them to obey, everything that He's commanded.
Tell them all about His love.

I will ever praise His name, for He's been so good to me.
Through all the raging storms,
He has calmed the wildest seas.
He has lifted me up and carried me through,
there's nothing He can't do.
So I'll take up my cross and set out on the road.

Go, therefore, and disciple all the nations.
Go, therefore, and disciple all the nations.
Teach them to obey, everything that He's commanded.
Tell them all about His love.

Chapter 15

By His Grace

      The freedom that comes in knowing Christ is immeasurable. When I accepted Christ as my personal Lord and Savior I was delivered, although I did not know it at the time. I knew that I was saved from eternal life in a real live place called hell. But, I did not realize to what extent I had received the power of the Holy Spirit to do anything that He would call me to do. It has been almost 20 years since I gave my heart to Christ, and I am still learning about the freedom I have in Him.

      Each and every one of us has a special purpose that God has given us the ability to fulfill. We must seek Him earnestly through Bible study and prayer and trust Him for His leadership and guidance. I have no doubt that if you want to know your purpose in life, God will give you discernment and wisdom as to what that purpose would be. I used to think that I had to be doing something big and wonderful for God and all people to notice. Not in a prideful way, but something that would make an impact on people. I did not believe I could live up to the standard I had put on myself in the work I did for the Lord.

So therefore, I would not try. I listened to the thoughts of self-doubt and figured that I was too timid and shy to do anything for the Lord. I did not *believe* I could be used by God that way. He is showing me more and more each day that I have it all wrong. He is showing me that His word is true.

"With God all things are possible."
Matthew 19:26, NKJV

    God is so faithful and so true to His character. He wants you as much as me to think outside the box. Do not limit God to what He can do in and through us. He is bigger than any obstacle we face. He has plenty of things He would like for us to do for Him, if we would just seek, ask, and listen. Then do it! I have often times left out one of those steps. One morning several years ago, I woke up and gave my day to the Lord. I had a good devotional time that morning and was charged and ready for the day. I can not remember every detail of that day, but I remember feeling Him near and I was in a very prayerful, praising mood.

    I was busy that morning and I went by the post office to get stamps. I stood in line, bought my stamps, and then went out into the lobby to prepare my envelopes for mailing. As I finished and dropped them in the slot to mail, an elderly lady came up to me and asked if I could help her a minute. I said, "Okay," and followed her to her post office box. It was at the top and her mail was wedged in it and she could not get it loose. I worked until I got it out then handed it to her. She thanked me and told me that she had problems with her fingers and she suffers from excruciating pain at times, I guess some form of arthritis or such. Anyhow, I told her that I was sorry to hear that and hoped she would feel better soon. As I turned to leave,

I stepped outside the door and I heard the Lord speak directly to my heart. He told me, *"Martha, go hold her hands and pray for her and her hands."* Imagine my surprise. I said, *"Lord, I can't do that, she will think I am a nut." "Go now." "I can't Lord, please forgive me."* I went on to my car and such strong conviction came over me. I knew without a doubt the Lord had spoken to me, but I let fear choke me, and now I wanted to go do what He told me.

So I got out of the car and went back inside. But she was already gone. I felt terrible and shameful that I did not listen to Him the first time. I went back to the car and prayed and asked the Lord for His forgiveness for my disobedience. I vowed to do what He says the first time, next time. I reminded myself of my own relationship to my children. Just like I discipline my children for obedience, my Heavenly Father did the same for me. It pains me to think that God may have used that time to heal the dear woman's hands, had I been obedient. Granted God could heal her, but I have no doubt He might have done it then. Not anything special I could do on my own, but that whole "being a willing servant" thing.

He longs to work through us. I refused to respond to what He was telling me to do because I felt as though I was not the right person for the job. I was not a preacher, teacher, or some great spiritual person; I was just me, timid and shy Martha. Now looking back I realize, that He had my heart that morning where He wanted it to be to hear from Him. He possibly wanted to do something extraordinary through an ordinary me.

The Father longs to do the same with you. He wants willing servants to be about His kingdom work. So with that all said, let me show you how neat He is. A few weeks later I was at home and the phone rang. It was a lady wanting to speak to my husband. She told me that she had a car for sale and wanted to know if my husband might be interested, she thought she was calling my father-n-law. I told her that she had the wrong number and gave her his number. She then asked if I thought that Jay might want to look at it. I told her I did not know, but I would ask him. I took her phone number and hung up.

Almost instantly, I sensed the Lord telling me to call her back and pray for her. I said in my mind, *"Oh, Lord, not again." "Are you sure you want me to do that?"* I need not wait for a reply. Nervous as can be, I picked up the phone and dialed, while praying for the boldness and words to pray. After a couple of rings she answered. I told her who I was and that the Lord wanted me to pray for her. I asked her if that was alright. She said, *"Yes"*, and I started praying for her. I do not even recall any of the words He had me pray, but I prayed. When I finished, she was crying. She went on to tell me that her husband had died just a few months prior and that it was his antique car she was trying to sell. She told me how lonely she was and that she had been praying and asking the Lord to help her and comfort her. When she finished, I was crying. I was so moved and thankful that I listened and this time obeyed the Father. He showed me that I can do it. All I needed to do is be willing.

He showed me first hand that I am as capable as the next person to be used by Him. I do not have to have a degree in theology to pray for someone. I do not have to be a preacher to share an encouraging message with them.

I do not have to be anything, but myself for God to use me. The Father didn't mark me useless when I failed to obey Him at the post office, He gave me another chance. God continues to give me tests of obedience and He will do the same for you. By His grace I am free to be what He's called me to be. You too dear friend have this same privilege. Get alone with God and start seeking His direction and plan for your life. Your purpose is a prayer away from being revealed to you by the Holy Spirit's leading.

By His Grace

By His grace I am free,
to be what He's called me to be.
Whether great or noble cause, or a friend to the lost.
I will serve with all my might,
until my spirit takes flight.
I can do all things through Christ
who gives me strength.

By His grace, I am saved.
All because of amazing grace.
I will firmly take my stand in the blessed promise land.
I will steady to the cause; of this world I'll have no fear.
I can do all things through Christ
who gives me strength.

Trials are hard in this life,
and at times hope seems drear,
But remember that the Lord has a plan.
A plan to grow and prosper you,
to make you more and more like Him
You can do all things through Christ
who strengthens you.

By His grace, I am saved.
All because of amazing grace.
I will firmly take my stand in the blessed promise land.
I will steady to the cause; of this world I'll have no fear.
I can do all things through Christ
who gives me strength.

Chapter 16

His Grace

It is funny that the Lord would have me write this chapter today of all days. I thought he would wait until a day when I was supercharged and full of zest for Him. But no, instead this has been a very difficult day and week for that matter. It is one of those days that I feel like all I am hanging from is that thread of grace. My husband is a self-employed do-it-yourself man, and with all this rainy weather plus a slow time of year, he is without work. This week makes the second week of no jobs. EEEKKK! We are into the middle of the month and few bills have been paid. So needless to say, I am a bit stressed. I know that the Lord will provide, for He has shown me numerous times that He can. But for some reason today, I am just plain tired.

As I sit here and reminisce of times past that His grace has abounded in my life, I am in awe. His grace was with me when my dad called us to his house and told us that he would no longer be taking his dialysis treatments. The doctor said he would probably live two or three weeks, he died two days later. His grace showed up when my son nearly died at six months of age from a rare intestinal problem. A freak occurrence was what they called it. His small intestine had backed into his large intestine, making it think food was being digested. He was in excruciating pain and great danger. They performed emergency surgery and repaired his intestines, as well as, removed his appendix to make scar tissue for the intestine to adhere to that it might not happen again. It was a very scary time for me and my husband and family.

That precious grace showed up when my mom was diagnosed with cancer. They found a nerve tumor on her chin bone, and she had a tonsil removed. The surgery was followed with six weeks of radiation. This all took place at the same time my son was born. I was recovering from a C-section and I couldn't stay with her. She was staying in Gainesville two hours away at the Hope Lodge while she had treatments. I missed her dearly and tried to go see her on weekends. It was a very intense time in my life as well as our entire family. She is cancer free today, praise God!

The next year a lady pulled out in front of me on a drizzly, rainy morning as I was on my way to work. I hit my brakes, but to no avail. I hit her at 55 mph, knocking her truck off its rear axle and sent her truck in one direction and tires in another. It totaled my car and scared me half to death, but we both walked away unscathed. It took me a couple of years to ease up on my brakes at intersections and relax. It has been five years since the accident and at times I still find myself hitting the brakes when someone comes up a side road.

These were very traumatic times for me, yet I had peace in the midst of them all. Something about that abundant, unexplainable, merciful grace can bring such sweet calm in the storm. I am not saying that I handled it with grace; I am saying that God's grace carried me.

At times I was mad, scared, even confused. But through them all, I knew He was there and that He was in control and that He knew just what I was going through and why.

But His grace does not just show up in extreme times. It has appeared on the days that I was unsure how my electric bill or house note would get paid. It appeared on the days that groceries were needed and money was not in excess. Even the grace that allows me to keep my big mouth shut when it needs to be shut. At times when I may have wanted to gossip; or if I am upset with my husband; or kids; or if friends have spoken something to me in confidence for prayer; He has helped me hold my tongue.

The grace that He gives so freely is not just for me. He gives it to each and every one of us. There is nothing that we can do to earn His grace, He just gives it. When I was going through all the trials I was not necessarily aware of the grace. I just went through each trial one day at a time. It was difficult and I wish I could say I was always happy and content and completely focused on God through it all. But I wasn't. I was scared, I was mad at times, and questioned God a lot through it all. But now looking back I can see the grace. And that is the way it probably is with you. You may be experiencing fiery trials and be questioning God and scared. But know that even when you can not see it, His grace is carrying you. If you are a child of God and have accepted Him as your personal Lord and Savior, then His grace He bestows on you.

The Bible reads:

> *"But God, who is rich in mercy, because of His great love with which He loved us, even when we were dead in trespasses, made us alive together in Christ (by grace you have been saved), and raised us up together, and made us sit together in the heavenly places in Christ Jesus, that in the ages to come He might show the exceeding riches of His grace in His kindness toward us in Christ Jesus. For by grace, you have been saved through faith, and that not of yourselves; it is the gift of God, not of works, lest anyone should boast. For we are His workmanship, created in Christ Jesus for good works, which God prepared beforehand that we should walk in them."*
> *Ephesians 2:4-10, NKJV*

Praise the Lord that we do not have to earn His grace or His love. He gave His life for us that we might know Him and experience His love and have eternal life with Him. I once heard an acronym for grace…

G-God's, **R**-Riches, **A**-At, **C**-Christ's, **E**-Expense

God gave His most treasured possession, for us. If God loved us so much that He gave Jesus to die for us on *our* cross, would He not provide our every need and love us deeply enough to bestow His marvelous grace on us. Yes, He loves us that much. I can not even begin to fathom that kind of unconditional love, yet I feel it everywhere I go. He loves you and me so much. His grace is sufficient for all that call upon His name. Praise God!

His Grace

*His grace is sufficient for me, His grace is sufficient for me,
He knows my every longing; He knows my every need,
His grace is sufficient for me.*

*He hears my every cry; He feels my every pain,
He knows every thought; He knows all my shame,
He loves me anyway; He cares all the same,
His grace is sufficient for me.*

*His grace is sufficient for me, His grace is sufficient for me,
He knows my every longing; He knows my every need,
His grace is sufficient for me.*

*I marvel at His love, that He so freely gives,
Unworthy of the gift, that He gave that I might live,
I shudder to even think, that He would die for me,
His grace is sufficient for me.*

*His grace is sufficient for me, His grace is sufficient for me,
He knows my every longing; He knows my every need,
His grace is sufficient for me.*

*Oh, let's raise our hands, and give Him all the praise,
Thank Him for His mercy; praise Him for His grace,
Lift up holy hands and give Him first place,
For mighty is His name, and sufficient is His grace.*

*His grace is sufficient for me, His grace is sufficient for me,
He knows my every longing; He knows my every need,
His grace is sufficient for me.*

114

Chapter 17

Come Unto Me

I find it hard to believe I am at this point. When I started this book, I questioned my ability to finish it. I have started and quit so many things in my life. But I would be lying if I told you that I wasn't extremely excited that I am finishing this book. God has worked in marvelous ways in my life through the writings of this book. I praise Him for seeing me through to completion. It is only by His grace and nudging I have been able to continue. Thank You Lord Jesus.

I have encountered much spiritual warfare while writing. There were days I wanted to throw my hands up and quit. Not just quit the book, but quit my marriage, quit my kids, quit my church, quit everything and just lie dormant until Jesus comes was what I wanted to do. Praise the Lord I didn't, His grace has been sufficient.

It has been several months since I have touched this book. God has been doing business in my heart and life. He has been refining me through many trials and tests. And I am glad to say that I am better for it. I fully believe He needed me to endure such things in order for me to be completely up front and straightforward in this chapter. I do not have my life all together by any means, nor would I even begin to tell you that you do not have yours together. But what I do know and can say without any hesitation is this: WE ALL NEED THE LORD JESUS CHRIST IN OUR LIVES AND HEARTS AS OUR PERSONAL LORD AND SAVIOR, AND WE NEED TO SEEK HIM DAILY IN PRAYER IN EVERY ASPECT OF OUR LIVES. Not one of us can survive without Christ. I know there are many people in the world who think they can, you may even be one of them. But those that believe this are dead wrong.

One day we will all have to stand before the Lord and give an account for everything we have done in our lives. If we are Christians, we will have to stand before Him and give an account for the things we have done, good or bad. And we will be judged for our unconfessed sins. It may be painful, it may be a relief, but it is inevitable, Heaven will be our destination. If you have never called on Christ and asked Him to be your personal Lord and Savior; you refuse to bow before Him and seek forgiveness and accept His salvation; my friend, your destination is eternity in a real place in a living hell, a place that never burns up. The Bible reads He will say, "I never knew you" (Matt. 7:21-23) cast them into the lake of fire. It will be too late to ask Him into your heart. No more chances. So many people deny that Christ even exists; they refuse to believe that it is as simple as it is to believe in Christ.

My hearts bleeds for those that refuse to believe. The end times are at hand and when He comes in all His glory, every knee *will* bow, and every tongue *will* confess that He is Lord. (Phil. 2:10) Even the vilest people, who laugh and mock and scream at the top of their lungs that there is no God, will bow and confess. It is written in the Bible plainly, and it *will* come to pass.

Dear friend, if this is you, I pray for you that you will pray and seek Him and find deliverance in Him. He loves you so very much. He longs for you to draw close to Him. He does not want to see any of us spend eternity in hell, but He gives us a free will to choose. He stands waiting to hear from you. It does not matter what your past is, it does not what matter what your present is, what does matter is where your future is. A beautiful, magnificent place with a mansion built just for you in Heaven by the Father Himself, or an eternity in a very literal place full of pain and agony and torment, a place where there will be no comfort, no rest? Not even the worst circumstances of this life on earth can compare to an eternity in hell. Jesus died that each one of us would have the opportunity for eternal life in Heaven. God's word says:

> *"For God so loved the world that He gave His one and only Son that whosoever believes in Him, would not perish, but have everlasting life."*
> *John 3:16*

God loves you, He loves me. That's it. He died on the cross for our sins. He took the sins of this world and died on a cross that was meant for us. He paid the ultimate price that we might live and trust in Him. He rose from the grave and ascended to Heaven and God sent a Comforter to us which is the Holy Spirit to dwell in the hearts of every man, woman, and child. When we were born, we were born with a corruptible seed of sin in our hearts. We are all sinners. When we ask Jesus into our hearts and seek His forgiveness, we die to our old man. God then plants the incorruptible seed of Jesus into our hearts, and raises us up in Christ. We become a new creation in Christ. When God looks upon us when we have Jesus in our hearts; He sees the blood of Jesus, covering our sins and us. Jesus died and purchased us with His precious blood that we might enter into Heaven and be joint heirs with Jesus. Dear friend, God wants so much to be a part of your life. Won't you let Him in? Are you tired? Are you weak and heavy laden? Come to Him, He will give you rest.

      You should know that satan would not want you to be sincere at this time, and he definitely does not want you to have one intimate moment with Christ. In fact he is shaking in his steps at the thought of one more person coming to a saving knowledge of Christ. Satan has no dominion over you, God is bigger than him. God is All-Powerful, satan is defeated. God is in control, satan is defeated. God has won the victory, SATAN IS DEFEATED! If you have asked Jesus into your heart and have a saving knowledge of Jesus, praise God. I ask you to join with me and pray that those that need to know Jesus will spend time with God and pray this prayer...

> *Gracious Father,*
>
> *I may not have lived the life You wanted me to live, but I come to You seeking forgiveness for all the sins that I have committed. I believe that You died on the cross for my sins, that You died and was buried, and that You rose again on the third day. I don't necessarily understand right now the magnitude of what you've done for me, but I am willing to learn. Save me Father from an eternity in hell, enter my heart and fill me with the Holy Spirit that I may grow closer to You and learn more about your ways. I ask these things in Jesus name,*
>
>   *Amen*

My friend if you just prayed this prayer, not only I but also every child of God rejoices for you. Not only us, but the Bible tells us that each time a soul is saved; the angels in Heaven rejoice and sing praises to His name. So at this very moment, angels are rejoicing over you. But most of all, Christ Himself is rejoicing for He knows that His life and death was not in vain. I praise God for you. Find yourself a church home, a God-fearing, Bible believing church, and tell them about your decision. They too will rejoice and will help disciple you in your new walk with the Lord.

Out of this entire book the most precious prayer to God and one that He will answer instantly is the prayer of His children who are seeking to have a personal relationship with Him. It is my desire that you find joy and peace and love in Christ Jesus today.

My Most Gracious Loving Father,

Thank you for Jesus. Thank you for giving Him to die on the cross for each one of us. Thank You for the souls that will seek You and find forgiveness and freedom in You. I lift up each and every dear child of yours who reads the pages of this book and ask You to bless them and fill them with the power of the Holy Spirit. I pray Your will would be done in and through their lives. I pray that You would use this book as an instrument to encourage others to come to You for anything. You are awesome Lord and All-Powerful and I know You can move mountains in each of these dear souls lives. Holy Spirit, rain down on them. And Father, most of all I pray for the dear children of Yours who will possibly read these pages and still refuse to call You Lord. Touch their hearts, soften them, and give them the ability to see their need for You.

You know who they are. I ask that they may find salvation in You before it is too late. And for all Your children who have asked You into their hearts, continue to guide them, comfort them, and meet them where they are at. Whatever struggles, battles, or debilitating circumstances they may be facing, be their strength, give them grace, be their peace. Allow them to grow through the trials and become more like You with each step they take. Your are God Almighty, King of Kings, and Lord of Lords, Our God reigns! In Christ wonderful and magnificent name, I ask these things, and I plead the blood of Jesus over each and every life be it Christian or non-Christian, that Your will would be done,   Amen

Come Unto Me

Come unto Me, ye who are weak and heavy laden, Come to Me.
Come unto Me, ye who are in need of a Savior, Come to Me.

I will lift you up to Heaven; I'll speak on your behalf.
I will tell my Father please, over look the past.
I bring a new creation, for all the world to see.
For when you look past the sinner, you're looking right at Me.

Come unto Me, ye who are weak and heavy laden, Come to Me.
Come unto Me, ye who are in need of a Savior, Come to Me.

Amazing grace how sweet the sound,
that saved a wretch like me.
He died that I might live, He rose to set me free.
I was lost but now I'm found, was blind but now I see,
I praise the Living Savior, I thank Him for Calvary.

Come unto Me, ye who are weak and heavy laden, Come to Me.
Come unto Me, ye who are in need of a Savior, Come to Me.

My friend have you felt, the tug upon your heart?
Is there shame in your past, do you ant a fresh start?
Then close your eyes and listen, for He's calling out your name.
Did you hear Him, did you hear Him say.....

Come unto Me, ye who are weak and heavy laden, Come to Me.
Come unto Me, ye who are in need of a Savior, Come to Me.

Dear Heavenly Father,
I recognize that I'm a sinner, in need of a Savior. I believe that you died and rose again, that I might have eternal life. Save me Lord today, enter my heart, I pray. In Jesus name, Amen

Come unto Me, ye who are weak and heavy laden, Come to Me.
Come unto Me, ye who are in need of a Savior, Come to Me.

About the Author

Martha Swindle has been married to her wonderful husband, Jay, for 17 years. They have three, beautiful children, Holly, Jay, and Jonathan, whom they have been home schooling for the past five years. She loves to sing, write songs, play the guitar, and make various craft projects. But first and foremost, she loves the Lord with all her heart. Her desire for this book is that it may bring its readers to a closer relationship to the Lord, to a saving knowledge of the One True Lord and Savior.

Martha has the gift of exhortation and encouragement and it comes across in the words of these pages, sometimes with humorous wit, other times with deep humility. Open and honest she shares her trials and triumphs through her own personal experiences of faith and perseverance. She challenges you in your daily walk and encourages you to experience God in your own daily walk through the avenue of prayer. Prayer is a must in our walk with the Lord and she opens up the box of fear and doubt and shares the simplicity of praying. A prayer is not a routine of fancy sounding words for all to hear and say… "Oh, doesn't he or she pray beautifully?" No, prayer is just a conversation between the one praying and God Most High. You speak, God listens. God speaks, you listen. Communion with the Father is a beautiful thing.

Martha has written several songs of faith. She is currently working on greeting cards and inspirational picture frames. She was presented with the "Best Poetry Award" at the 2005 Florida Christian Writer's Conference for lyrics from some of her songs.

124

Quiet Moments

Quiet Moments

Quiet Moments

Quiet Moments